The
HIDDEN PLACES
of
NOTTINGHAMSHIRE

Edited by
Joanna Billing

Published by:

Travel Publishing Ltd

7a Apollo House, Calleva Park

Aldermaston, Berks, RG7 8TN

ISBN 1-902-00706-9

© Travel Publishing Ltd 1998

First Published:	1991
Second Edition:	1995
Third Edition:	1998

Regional Titles in *the Hidden Places* Series:

Channel Islands	Devon & Cornwall
Dorset, Hants & Isle of Wight	East Anglia
Gloucestershire	Heart of England
Lancashire & Cheshire	Lake District & Cumbria
Northeast Yorkshire	Northumberland & Durham
Nottinghamshire	Peak District
Potteries	Somerset
South East	South Wales
Surrey	Sussex
Thames & Chilterns	Welsh Borders
Wiltshire	Yorkshire Dales

National Titles in *the Hidden Places* Series:

England	Ireland
Scotland	Wales

Printing by: Nuffield Press, Abingdon

Cartography by: Estates Publications, Tenterden, Kent

Line Drawings: Sarah Bird

Editor: Joanna Billing

Cover : Clare Hackney

Born in 1961, Clare was educated at West Surrey College of Art and Design as well as studying at Kingston University. She runs her own private water-colour school based in Surrey and has exhibited both in the UK and internationally. The cover is taken from an original water-colour of Newstead Abbey.

Foreword

The Hidden Places series is a collection of easy to use travel guides taking you, in this instance, on a relaxed but informative tour through the beautiful countryside, forests and industrial heartland of Nottinghamshire. Our books contain a wealth of interesting information on the history, the countryside, the towns and villages and the more established places of interest in the county. But they also promote the more secluded and little known visitor attractions and places to stay, eat and drink many of which are easy to miss unless you know exactly where you are going.

We include hotels, inns, restaurants, public houses, teashops, various types of accommodation, historic houses, museums, gardens, garden centres, craft centres and many other attractions throughout Nottinghamshire. Most places have an attractive line drawing and are cross-referenced to coloured maps found at the rear of the book. We do not award merit marks or rankings but concentrate on describing the more interesting, unusual or unique features of each place with the aim of making the reader's stay in the local area an enjoyable and stimulating experience.

Whether you are visiting Nottinghamshire for business or pleasure or in fact are living in the county we do hope that you enjoy reading and using this book. We are always interested in what readers think of places covered (or not covered) in our guides so please do not hesitate to use the reader reaction forms provided to give us your considered comments. We also welcome any general comments which will help us improve the guides themselves. Finally if you are planning to visit any other corner of the British Isles we would like to refer you to the list of other *Hidden Places* titles to be found at the rear of the book.

Contents

CHAPTER ONE
Nottingham and Southwest Nottinghamshire

Nottingham Castle Gatehouse

Chapter 1 - Area Covered

For precise location of places please refer to the colour maps found at the rear of the book.

● East Retford

● Worksop

● Mansfield Woodhouse

● Mansfield

NOTTINGHAMSHIRE

● Sutton in Ashfield

Newark on Trent ●

● Kirkby in Ashfield

● Hucknall

● Arnold

● NOTTINGHAM

● Beeston

1
Nottingham and Southwest Nottinghamshire

Introduction

The county of Nottinghamshire, in the north Midlands, lies mainly on the low ground basin of the River Trent between the peaks of Derbyshire and south Yorkshire and the lowlands of Lincolnshire. A county of contrasts: Nottinghamshire has plenty of industry but it has also retained much of its rural heritage as well as the remains of the famous Forest of Sherwood.

The county town, Nottingham, lies in the southwestern corner of Nottinghamshire and is, by far, the largest town. A lively mix of the old and new, Nottingham has a colourful history which spans the ages - from Anglo-Saxon times when it was founded by a tribal chief called Snot to the industrial expansion of the 19th century. Today, this blend of ancient and modern makes Nottingham a place worthy of exploration.

Perhaps best known for its past, anyone coming to the city is sure to visit its famous castle. But those expecting to walk down dark, dank passageways in the footsteps of the evil Sheriff of Nottingham will be disappointed as the castle seen today was built much later and in less uncertain times. The old castle, which played such a part in the many films dedicated to the legend of Robin Hood, was already in a state of disrepair by the time of the Civil War and was destroyed soon afterwards. However, the legendary tales of the outlaw hero and his merry band of followers is still very much alive in the city.

The Industrial Revolution saw the mechanisation of the lace and hosiery industries of which Nottingham was a centre and many of the surrounding towns and villages dependent. Mills sprang up in the towns, taking the industry out of the home and causing many families to migrate from their villages to find work in the mills. Coal, which played such an important role in this mechanisation programme, had been mined for many years to the west of Nottingham but, after the mid-19th century, the scale of the mining operations expanded dramatically. Thus the nature of the area changed: the towns grew, with quickly built rows of terraced housing for the new factory and mill workers, and the rural villages lost many of their inhabitants. Today, however, something of a reversal is taking place with many people, working in the city, moving out into the villages to the south of Nottingham to find a quieter home life.

Nottingham

Nottingham, the self-proclaimed Queen of the Midlands, is justifiably said to be one of England's finest cities. It is ripe for exploration but visitors are regaled with the Robin Hood theme wherever they go. However, there is much more to this fascinating city than the legend of the people's outlaw: an interesting and ancient history, fine architecture, and many unusual attractions make this an ideal start to anyone's discovery of the county.

The settlement of Nottingham was founded by the unfortunately named Snot, chief of a 6th-century Anglo-Saxon tribe. He and his people carved out dwellings in the soft local sandstone and the settlement thrived to become Snottingaham - home of the followers of Snot. The name changed into its currently more acceptable form at some stage in Nottingham's ancient history but when that was has never been established.

Commanding an imposing position, high above the city centre and situated on a rocky outcrop, **Nottingham Castle** is an excellent place from which to begin any tour of the city. However, those looking for the famous castle which features so heavily in the tales of Robin Hood will be sorely disappointed as the buildings seen today date from after the English Civil War and precious little remains of the original fortification.

The original castle was built after the Battle of Hastings by William the Conqueror and William Peveril as part of the king's general fortification of many strategically important sites. Its elevated position, overlooking the city and the River Trent, made Nottingham Castle one of the foremost castles in Norman England and it played host to many important visitors. Of a typical Norman motte and bailey design, the stone walls are thought to have been added in the early 12th century and it was further fortified by Henry II. Nottingham Castle's heyday came in the 14th and 15th centuries however, when, not only was King David II of Scotland held prisoner here for a while in around 1346 but, in the mid-15th century, Edward IV proclaimed himself king from Nottingham Castle and, later, his brother, Richard III, built new state apartments and lived at the castle for most of his reign.

Thereafter, though, the castle gradually fell into disrepair until Charles I came to Nottingham in 1642 and raised his standard at the castle at the start of the Civil War. Unfortunately, the king found little support for his cause in the city and he moved on to Shrewsbury, leaving the castle in the hands of the Parliamentarians. Over the course of the war, the Royalists made several attempts to recapture the castle but Cromwell's supporters held out. After the fighting was over the castle building was rendered uninhabitable and it was finally demolished in 1674 by the Duke of Newcastle who went on to build his palace on the site.

Today, the duke's palace, rebuilt after it was ramsacked by supporters of the Reform Bill in 1831, is home to the **Castle Museum**. However, visitors here are still able to see some of the remains of the original castle. The 13th-century gatehouse, though much restored, is still standing and parts of the moat and outer bailey can be seen. The museum, when it was opened by the Prince of Wales in 1878, was also the first municipal art gallery in the country outside London and, today, the collection is particularly noted for its fine selection of Victorian paintings. The museum has a fine collection of silverware and ceramics and the Story of Nottingham, a mix of displays and audio visual presentations, is well worth a visit. Besides the Castle Museum, is the **Sherwood Foresters Regimental Museum**, which continues the castle's connections with the military. The regiment was first raised in 1741 and, among the many displays, there is an area dedicated to the Nottingham flying ace of World War I, Captain Albert Ball, VC. He died in 1917, at the age of 20, having shot down 43 enemy aircraft and a statue has been erected in his memory which can be seen in the castle grounds.

At the base of Castle Rock lies the famous **Trip to Jerusalem Inn** where the crusaders are said to have stopped for a pint to fortify themselves before their long journey to the Holy Land. Dating back to around 1189, it is said to be the oldest pub in England. Set back into the sandstone rock, the building was once the brewhouse for the castle and from here travellers to the Holy Land bought their ale. In the pub's cellars is Mortimer's Hole, a cave hewn out of the sandstone rock which leads to the castle. It is through this passageway that Edward III crept to capture Roger Mortimer. Later sentenced to death, Mortimer's ghost is said to haunt the cave.

Trip to Jerusalem Inn

Also at the base of Castle Rock and housed in a terrace of four 17th-century cottages is the ***Brewhouse Yard Museum***. Depicting the life of the people of the city up to the 1990s, the museum has accurately furnished rooms as well as a series of shops: from a Victorian kitchen to shop window displays from the 1920s.

Opposite the Trip to Jerusalem Inn is a charming medieval building that is home the ***Lace Centre***. As well as holding lace making demonstrations, there is also a vast selection of high quality lace available for purchase. A fine example of a timber framed house of around 1450, the building itself was moved from its original site on Middle Pavement in 1968. Not far away and set in the heart of Nottingham's historic Lace Market, is the ***Lace Hall***, housed in a restored chapel. Here the story of Nottingham's famous industry is told, from the days when it was a cottage craft through to mechanisation and the days of the great textile factories. Visitors can not only see some of the giant machines which produced the delicate material but also see various types of lace being made.

Continuing with the theme of textiles, the ***Museum of Costume and Textiles***, in Castle Gate, contains a fine collection of costumes from 1790 to the mid-20th century, all displayed in period rooms. There are also many other exhibits on show including tapestries; knitted, woven, and printed textiles; and fashion accessories through the ages. The museum is housed in a terrace of brick houses that was constructed, in 1788, by Cornelius Launder, a former High Sheriff. Castle Gate is an interesting street in itself and well worth a second look. The entrance to the museum has one of the finest examples of a door case and fanlight to be seen in the area and whilst Number 57, almost opposite the museum, is much simpler, the building has a stuccoed front to bring it in line with the rest of the street.

Lace Centre

Further down Castle Gate is ***Newdigate House*** built in a refined fashion in 1680 though its wrought iron screen and gates date from the early 18th century. The house now forms part of the United Services Club and it was, between 1705 and 1711, the home of Marshall Tallard, commander of the defeated French army at the Battle of Blenheim in 1704.

The present red brick building of ***St Nicholas' Church*** replaces the medieval church which stood here until 1643 and the days of the Civil War. It was from this church's tower that Royalists fired upon the castle in an attempt to regain control and, after the attack, the Parliamentarian governor of the castle ordered the church's destruction so no further attacks could take place. Rebuilding the church was completed in 1682 and, inside, at the east end of the south aisle, there is a tombstone to Lawrence Collin, the master gunner of the castle during the Civil War.

Beneath Broad Marsh Centre, one of the city's major shopping precincts, lies the **Caves of Nottingham**, a popular attraction which opened in 1994. The city is built on sandstone and throughout Nottingham's history the rock has been tunnelled to provide first shelter and then hiding places. Now, thanks to local voluntary groups, these man-made caves have been saved for future generations. The most spectacular cave in the system, the Pillar Cave, dates back to 1250 and it now features the remains of the country's only underground tannery. During the Middle Ages, the city was an important leather producer but the caves were also commonly used as pub cellars: the constant temperature being ideal for the storage of beer

Caves of Nottingham

and wine. Most recently, the caves were used as air raid shelters during the blitz of World War II and one of the caves has been left as a reminder to those more recent, desperate times.

Nearby, is the city's **Galleries of Justice** and the unusual and interesting attraction of justice 19th-century style. Condemned, a major crime and punishment experience, allows visitors to put themselves in the place of an accused in the harsh days around 1833. Cramped cells, capital punishment, and the possibility of transportation to the New World were the lot of a hapless criminal in those days and their discomfort is made very real by the restored period settings.

Found near the bottom of High Pavement is Nottingham's largest parish church: **St Mary's Church** is also, probably, the city's oldest as it appears to have been founded in Saxon times. However, today's church dates from the 15th century though there are some 19th- and early 20th-century additions which include windows by a series of renowned stained glass makers. Also inside is a Bishop's Throne carved in 1890, when it was thought that the church would become the cathedral for the diocese of Southwell.

Though no market has been held here since the 1920s, the vast expanse of the **Old Market Square** is still lies at the centre of the life of Nottingham and it is now surrounded by all the usual high street shops. Nottingham is particularly famous for its **Goose Fair** which gained this name from the large flocks of geese that were sold here around Michaelmas. Mentioned in a charter dated 1284, the Goose Fair is still held today on the first Thursday in October.

On the edge of The Park, an old royal hunting ground that was developed for housing in 1827, stands the Roman Catholic cathedral of **St Barnabas**. Built in 1841 by Pugin, the exterior is rather severe although the spire is very fanciful. Inside, much of Pugin's original decoration has been replaced though his stained glass windows remain in the aisle.

Nottingham's links with the legend and tales of Robin Hood are well known and, for those interested in the story, a visit to **The Tales of Robin Hood** is well worth while. The life of the outlaw is told through a series of historically accurate displays, from his imprisonment by the Sheriff of Nottingham to feasting in Sherwood Forest. After a tour, by chair ride, visitors can then look at the history of the legend and also learn of the detective work undertaken in the 1930s to authenticate the legend.

As in many other industrial towns, the late 18th century saw the building of canals to serve the expanding populations and aid the transportation of goods. Nottingham was no exception and, in 1796, the **Nottingham Canal** was completed, thus linking the town with many of the country's more well-known waterways. Almost 15 miles in length and rising, by a series of 20 locks, some 130 feet, the canal ran from the River Trent, through the centre of Nottingham, to the Cromford Canal at Langley Mill, in neighbouring Derbyshire. Today only some 7 miles and three locks are left but this does include the stretch through the city. A walk along the banks of the canal may not be one of the county's most scenic trails but it does give a very good insight into the life of Nottingham in the last century and there is also much of interest to those who revel in industrial archaeology.

Along the Nottingham Canal, and still with its own basin found under an arch for easy loading and unloading, is the **Canal Museum**. Dating from the mid-19th century, this four storey building was the warehouse for one of the largest firms of canal carriers, Fellows, Morton, and Clayton. The firm went into liquidation in 1948 and this magnificent building has been restored and refurbished to house many displays and models which illustrate the history of the Trent Valley. The story, from rise to decline, of the country's network of canals and navigable waterways is also told and includes a reconstruction of an area of the warehouse as it would have appeared in its heyday.

Canal Museum, Nottingham

The suburb of **Lenton**, just to the west of the city centre, is an ancient settlement, which takes its name from the River Leen and ton or tun meaning enclosed place, that certainly existed in Anglo-Saxon times. However, it is the Middle Ages which saw the most prosperous times for Lenton. Then, its fair which lasted several days rivalled those of Nottingham but it is the great Cluniac **Priory** which dominated the history of the town. Founded in the early 12th century by William Peveril, it was, until dissolution at the hands of Henry VIII in the 16th century, one of the country's most influential priories as well as one of the wealthiest. Today, little can be seen of the priory buildings but, at the bottom of Old Church Street can be found the base of a stone pillar which is believed to have been part of the processional way behind the high altar of the priory church. Excavations opposite the pillar base in 1977 uncovered the some of the foundations of the Lady Chapel as well as a human skeleton.

The Bell Inn, which lies in the heart of the city, is one of the oldest inns in Nottingham and is also believed to be one of the oldest in the county: scholars at Nottingham University have traced it back to 1437. Skipping through some 450 years, in 1898, the premises were bought by Joseph Jackson and this famous pub has remained in the family ever since.

Today, the Bell Inn is run by David who is ably assisted by two of his four sons, Richard and Paul. This is very much a family run establishment and the superb interior, every corner of which has a story to tell, reflects perfectly the age of the building. However, what really makes a trip to the Bell Inn special, is the wonderful ale and

The Bell Inn

food served here that is hard to equal. Real ales are very much order of the day with an ever changing range from which to choose. Whilst the bar area is downstairs, upstairs there is a wonderful restaurant that is well worth a visit. *The Bell Inn, 18 Angel Row, Old Market Square, Nottingham NG1 6HL Tel: 0115 947 5241*

Situated on Canal Street, next to the Canal Museum and near the Chesterfield Canal, is the interestingly named **Fellows, Morton, and Clayton** public house and restaurant. Once the heart of the town's busy canal transport business, this was a bustling place and the many of the old warehouses and associated office buildings have been restored and they make an unusual and attractive area to visit. Fellows, Morton, and Clayton were the Pickfords of their day, a firm of canal hauliers and the pub now occupies their old office building; the restaurant, The Wharf, is in the old stables. This magnificent listed building, in the summer, is decorated with a colourful display of hanging baskets and tubs which have, for the past four years, won the pub first prize in the Nottingham in Bloom competition. It is a truly wonderful sight and well worth seeing.

Inside, the pub and restaurant are equally attractive. The old buildings have retained many of their original features and, with plenty of canal memorabilia adorning the walls, this is a place full of character. There are high ceilings and a spiral staircase leads up to the dining area on a mezzanine level. Jennifer and Les came here at the beginning of 1990 and they have made this one of the most popular venues in Nottingham. Open all day, everyday, the menu of delicious meals and tasty snacks is complemented by the additional dishes to be found on the specials board. Above the bar area there is still a brewhouse where, at present, two ales are brewed and Jennifer and Les are happy to show any interested visitors around. *Fellows, Morton, and Clayton, 54 Canal Street, Nottingham NG1 7EH Tel: 0115 950 6795*

Fellows, Morton, and Clayton

Hotel Des Clos offers guests a peaceful haven away from the hustle and bustle of the late 20th century whilst also offering guests

Hotel Des Clos

the latest modern comfort. Situated only five minutes drive from the centre of Nottingham, this family run hotel lies just yards from the River Trent in quiet and secluded country surroundings. Originally a series of Victorian farm buildings, the hotel's owner, John, converted the derelict buildings into this magnificent establishment centred around a courtyard packed with colourful pots of flowers.

John Abbey is not only the proud owner of Hotel Des Clos but is also an excellent chef and guests will be treated to a wonderful dinner in either the charming dining room or, if the weather is fine, outside on the picturesque paved courtyard. To complement the lunch and dinner menus there is a comprehensive wine cellar which boasts one of the finest French wine lists in the country.

This is a first class establishment and, as might be expected, the guest accommodation is of an equally high standard. All the 10 bedrooms are individually decorated and furnished and each as a luxury en-suite bathroom. *Hotel Des Clos, Old Lenton Lane, Nottingham NG7 2SA Tel: 0115 986 6566 Fax: 0115 986 0343*

One of the city's premier attractions, ***The Sheriff's Lodge*** offers everyone a night out with a difference. From the outside, the Victorian schoolhouse does not look too promising but once inside

guests enter the world of the Middle Ages. To be more precise, the year is 1193; King Richard is away fighting in the Crusades, Prince John is on the throne as Prince Regent, and the evil Sheriff of Nottingham is having a banquet. These banquets are held each Friday and Saturday evening and guests are treated to an authentic medieval meal accompanied by the finest English ales and ciders. Medieval dress is available for hire but it is by no means essential.

Throughout the evening a band of professional actors entertain the guests with traditional old English music, juggling, and jesting and, for those wishing to start the evening with a pre-dinner drink, there is Lizzie's Tavern. Also decorated and refurbished in a medieval style, the Tavern is

The Sheriff's Lodge the perfect place to get into the right mood for the evening ahead. The Sheriff's Lodge also holds other themed nights including Victorian evenings, World War II dinners, and special children's events. Facilities for the disabled are excellent and there is ample car parking. *The Sheriff's Lodge, 162-176 Canal Street, Nottingham NG1 7HG Tel: 0115 924 0088 Fax: 0115 948 0333*

Close to the Canal Museum and on the banks of the Beeston stretch of the Trent and Mersey Canal is the **Navigation Inn**. This old building dates back the days of canal travel itself and was once the lock house for the lock that stands right at the back of the pub. The original rings that were used for tethering the horses are still in place and next door is the old stables. This is a very busy stretch of canal and also one of Nottingham's great tourist attractions, so the Navigation Inn is well placed to offer those walking the towpath refreshment.

Navigation Inn

As well as having plenty of seating outside on the canal bank, the interior of the inn not only has more comfortable seating but also an interesting collection of old pictures on the walls. Naturally, these all have a canal and boating theme, to bring back the old days of the bargees, but there is also the odd stuffed fish and knotted rope to be seen. As well as offering a range of real ales, the Navigation Inn also serves bar snacks at lunchtime. *Navigation Inn, 6 Wilford Street, Nottingham NG2 1AA Tel: 0115 941 7139*

Around Nottingham

Arnold
Map 3 ref C6

3 miles N of Nottingham on B684

On the outskirts of Nottingham, this once separate town is now more a suburb of the expanding city. Like many towns and villages around Nottingham, Arnold was very much part of the local lace and hosiery industry and, in 1860, the firm I and R Morley built their factory here. Still standing today, though the company ceased operation in 1963, **Morley's Hosiery Factory** is a fine example of mid-Victorian industrial architecture. Two storeys high, with eight bays and a large central clock, an elaborate extension of three storeys was added in 1885.

In the centre of the town can be found an ideal indoor playarea for younger children. **Tumble Town**, complete with climbing frames, bouncing castles, and helter-skelters, offers a safe place for children to let off steam in a supervised environment.

However, there is some pleasant countryside to the north and east of the centre of Arnold where, too, can be found ***Burntstump Country Park***. Covering some 65 acres, the park has plenty of open space for picnics and games as well as woodlands of beech, oak, and birch. Visitors in late spring will also be able to admire the rhododendrons.

The Burnt Stump was formerly a game keeper's cottage on the old Bestwood Hall estate and it is still within the boundaries of Sherwood Forest. As might be imagined from its position, the pub is surrounded by mature trees and there is also a lovely oval village cricket pitch right outside. An excellent family pub, there is plenty of space outside to sit and enjoy a drink, whilst the children can play safely in their own purpose built area.

The Burnt Stump

As well as coming here to sample the wonderful ales on offer, The Burnt Stump is also a very popular place for lunch and dinner, particularly at weekends when it is advisable to book. Carefully decorated and comfortably furnished, the pub's interior is made all the more pleasant by the veranda windows which overlook the paved patio outside. *The Burnt Stump, Burnt Stump Hill, Arnold, Nottinghamshire NG5 9PQ Tel: 0115 963 1508*

Greenwood Bonsai Studio is a rare and fascinating place in the outskirts of Arnold, on the A614. Run by Harry and Petra and their son Corin, this unique family business has something to interest everyone. It is one of the largest established bonsai centres in the world and really has to be seen to be believed.

Set in over 12 acres of lovely countryside (three and a half of which are open to the public) everything to do with bonsai can be found here, from seedlings and cultivars to exclusive bonsai containers and information books. Harry and Petra are both internationally known and respected; Harry as a bonsai artist, lecturer, and author and Petra as a bonsai and ceramic artist who makes beautiful, handcrafted bonsai containers. Outside, the extensive nursery area is Corin's domain, whilst in the main studio there is a

Greenwood Bonsai Studio

magnificent bonsai display and a separate studio where regular lectures and demonstrations are given. *Greenwood Bonsai Studio, Greenwood Gardens, Ollerton Road, Arnold, Nottinghamshire NG5 8PR Tel: 0115 920 5757*

Gedling

Map 3 ref C6

3 miles NE of Nottingham off the A612

Now very much a suburb of the city, the village of Gedling dates back to before the days of the Norman Conquest when it was known as Ghellinge. Whilst he was building the first castle at Nottingham, William Peveril (whom many believe to be William the Conqueror's illegitimate son) was also given 10 acres of land in the village to make an orchard by the king. The orchard survived until the 20th century but is no longer visible today.

Though coal was been mined in the village since the Middle Ages it was the sinking of two shafts in Bell field in 1900, as well as the earlier arrival of the railway in 1846, which turned Gedling from a rural village into a bustling suburb. Gedling colliery did not last long as it was one of the first pits to be closed, in 1933, when much of the mining industry of Nottinghamshire was cut back.

Sneiton

Map 3 ref B7

1 mile E of Nottingham on the A612

This suburb of Nottingham is, perhaps, best remembered as the birthplace, in 1829, of William Booth, the founder of the Salvation Army. The small terraced house, where he and his family lived until 1831, is still standing in Notintone Place and, in front of the building, is a statue of the great man. Now home to the **Museum to William Booth**, which is part of the William Booth Memorial Complex, it is open by appointment only.

After his father's death, Booth's mother was forced to move to Goosegate, Nottingham where she kept a shop selling toys and sewing materials and it was whilst in the area that Booth first saw the appalling conditions in which many people lived in the 19th century. At the age of 16, William Booth gave his first sermon in a house in Kid Street and it was just a year later that he became a Methodist preacher. In 1849, Booth left Nottingham for London and became a Methodist minister but, finding the church structures to constraining, he started, in 1865, the Christian Missions which, in 1878, became the Salvation Army. Working in some of the most deprived areas of the capital, Booth and his Salvation Army workers were the subject of persecution and, in some cases, violent behaviour. Yet, despite this the following 10 years saw the movement spread to all corners of the world, including America, Australia, and South Africa. In 1905, William Booth was made a freeman of the city of Nottingham, seven years before his death in 1912.

One unusual landmark on the skyline of this suburb and that of Nottingham is **Greens Mill**, a five storey brick tower mill dating from 1807. Now beautifully restored after becoming derelict earlier this century as well as suffering from fire damage in 1947, the mill is back in working order. The mill was built by George Green, a prosperous Nottingham baker, but it was his son, also called George, who really left his mark. Without any formal education after the age of nine, George went on to become one of country's leading early 19th-century scientists and mathematicians. Although George died in 1841, at the age of 48, many of his techniques are still applied today. In tribute to Sneiton's other famous son, the buildings adjacent to the mill contain a **Science Centre**, with interactive displays on computers, lasers, ultrasonics, and magnetism.

Colwick   Map 3 ref C7
2 miles E of Nottingham on A612

A large area, some 250 acres, around old gravel workings has been converted into **Colwick Country Park**, where, as well as expanses of water offering facilities for sailing, rowing, and fishing, there is also a nature reserve. This country park was once part of the estate surrounding Colwick Hall, which is now a hotel. Originally the home of the Byron family, the ornate country house came into the hands of the Muster family in the 17th century. Though a private family house for much of its life, the hall has seen some turbulent times including, in 1831, being the scene of looting and rioting by an angry mob.

Holme Pierrepont   *Map 3 ref C7*
3 miles E of Nottingham off A52

Although Holme has been in the hands of the Pierrepont family since 1284, the present **Holme Pierrepont Hall** only dates from the early 16th century but it remains one of the best examples of a brick built house in the county. Open to the public on a restricted timetable, the hall is well worth a visit as, not only have some of the ground floor rooms been restored to their original state and furnished in the style of the early 17th century, but also, the ceiling of one of the first floor bedrooms has been removed to reveal the impressive roof construction.

Also worthy of a visit is **St Edmond's Church** situated adjacent to the hall. The home of several interesting Pierrepont family monuments, including a 14th-century brass to an unknown lady, the church retains some features of the original 13th-century building although the exterior is 19th century.

However, these days, Holme Pierrepont is more widely known as the home of the **National Watersports Centre**. Built to Olympic standards, there is a full size rowing course and a wild water slalom course, all man-made from the pasture and quarries which once dominated the area. The planting of trees and shrubs to landscape the whole site has ensured that there is plenty on and off the water for those not quite up to world class competition.

Edwalton   *Map 3 ref C7*
3 miles S of Nottingham on A606

The village takes its name from a Saxon settler, Eadweald, who was responsible for reclaiming the surrounding land from the marshes. Though the village has grown in size, due to its close proximity to the centre of Nottingham, the main street still retains some village charm.

Once a farming village, many of the old buildings have been converted into houses and bungalows and the old post office and school house can still be seen next to the church. Built in around 1166, the church is believed to have been constructed by a knight as penance for his part in the murder of Thomas á Becket. The chancel, however, had to be rebuilt in the 17th century after it had collapsed and the tower is unusual in that it was built during the reign of Mary I, Henry VIII's eldest daughter.

Edwalton is a place well worth visiting for anyone interested in flowers and gardening as is it the home of Wheatcrofts, the internationally renowned rose growers.

West Bridgford
Map 3 ref C7

2 miles S of Nottingham on A60

This town, now very much a suburb of Nottingham, lies across the River Trent from the rest of the city and it is home to the famous Trent Bridge test and county cricket ground as well as the home of Nottingham Forest Football Club.

The Old Colonial, in this pleasant south Nottingham suburb, is a recent, purpose built pub that manages, very successfully, to blend the old with the new. Set in well laid out, landscaped gardens, where there is plenty of outdoor seating, the attractive building incorporates many features from much older establishments. A riot of colour in the summer, the distinctive Old Colonial is decked out with numerous flower-filled hanging baskets.

The Old Colonial

The story is the same inside the pub: the first class, modern interior is decorated and comfortably furnished to produce the character and charm of a bygone age. The Old Colonial has an excellent range of ales and it also has a comprehensive menu which allows customers a wide degree of choice. Open all day, every day, this pub is a great place to bring children as there are special areas for the family as well as no smoking sections. *The Old Colonial, Compton Acres, West Bridgford, Nottinghamshire NG2 7PA Tel: 0115 945 5573*

Wollaton
Map 3 ref B7

2 miles W of Nottingham on A609

Built in the 1580s to the designs of Robert Smythson, who is famous for designing Harwick Hall in Derbyshire, *Wollaton Hall* was the home of the Willoughby family. Francis Willoughby, head of the family at that time, had made his money from his ownership of the local coal mines and he wanted to construct a grand and lavish house. However, the grandiose building plans coupled with losses incurred by some of his other business interests nearly bankrupted the family. Fortunately, the extravagant front façade of classical columns, busts of philosophers and mythological characters, and flamboyant gables remains.

Wollaton Hall

The hall now houses many items of interest though only three rooms have been restored to their former grandeur: the great hall, the entrance hall, and a beautiful salon. The building is also home to the *Natural History Museum* which is based on the collection of Francis Willoughby who was a noted naturalist of the mid-17th century and a friend of John Ray. Meanwhile, the hall's outbuildings have been transformed into the *Nottingham Industrial Museum* and the city's major industries are all represented. There are bicycles, from boneshakers and penny-farthings through to Raleigh and Humber models, and the progression to the motorcycle is given space in the form of the Brough machines of the 1920s and 1930s. It was whilst riding a Brough motorcycle that TE Lawrence had his fatal crash in 1935. Textiles, and particularly stocking frames and knitting machines, can be found here as can machinery from the pharmaceutical industry. Finally, the local coal mines are also represented and there is a particularly fine example of a horse winding gin from 1844 on display in the courtyard.

Martin's Pond, thought to be the first nature reserve opened in a city, was probably a medieval fishpond belonging to Wollaton Hall and, in the surrounding land, over 150 species of flowering plants and 70 species of birds have been recorded. Nearby **Harrison's Plantation**, which is also managed by the Nottinghamshire Wildlife Trust, is an area of mixed woodland which dates back to the 18th century.

Several prize fighters have been born and bred in Nottinghamshire and Wollaton was the home of John Shaw. Contesting only two prize fights, John was probably the least known and he died, in 1815, of wounds he sustained whilst fighting with the Lifeguards at the Battle of Waterloo.

Strelley
Map 3 ref B6

4 miles NW of Nottingham off A6002

Though the village lies close to the centre of Nottingham, Strelley still retains several cottages that were built for workers on the Strelley Hall estate. The manor of Strelley goes back to Norman times and was once held by Ralph Edge, who, on three occasions, was elected Lord Mayor of Nottingham in the 17th century. The village church, originally dating from the 13th century, has some fine monuments to the local de Strelley family, the original lords of the manor, whilst its well preserved 15th-century rood screen is exceptionally tall and slender.

Oldmoor Wood, planted in the late 18th century to provide timber and cover for game, is now a small broad-leaved wood which provides an excellent habitat for woodpeckers, jays, and redpolls as well as moths and butterflies.

The Broad Oak Inn

In the heart of peaceful Strelley lies **The Broad Oak Inn** which dates back to the 17th century. Then it was owned by the Edge family who also owned much of the village itself but, times have changed, and now the pub is managed by Hazel and Brent. Attractive from the outside, the Broad Oak is named after the magnificent oak tree which stands on the lawn at the front of the pub and, in its shade, there are numerous tables and chairs. There is also a play area for children who are most welcome to join the rest of the family at the Broad Oak.

Inside, much of the original character and charm of this old pub has been retained along with the huge beams and old fire places. These come into their own in the winter months when fires roar away in the grates. As well as being renowned for the excellent beer, including Kimberley Classic and Kimberley Cool, the Broad Oak is fast gaining a reputation for the delicious meals that are served here every day. *The Broad Oak Inn, Main Street, Strelley, Nottinghamshire NG8 6PD Tel: 0115 929 3340*

Bulwell *Map 3 ref B6*

3 miles N of Nottingham on B682

Originally the whole area surrounding the village was covered by forest and it is probable that the settlement took its name from a spring in the old woodland. However, a local legend tells the story of the naming of the village rather differently: it was an enraged bull which gored a rock here from which a spring flowed. Clearance of the forest and the cultivation of the released land began as early as the days of the Normans and, by the 13th century, villagers were given the rights to graze their sheep and cattle on the land.

Life in this small rural farming village remain relatively unchanged for many years until the coming of the Industrial Revolution in the 18th century. The nearby River Leen, on which the village stands, was utilised as a power source and used to drive cotton mills as well as providing the means to carry out many of the processes needed in the hosiery and lace industries. By the mid-19th century industrial fervour was at its greatest and the sinking of both the Cinderhill and Bulwell pits, in the 1840s, ensured the growth of the town. In 1877, this once quiet village was accepted as an large, industrial borough of the city of Nottingham.

The history of Bulwell is typical of many villages that expanded at the time of the Industrial Revolution and much of the building work here dates from the mid to late 19th century. Those familiar with the film version of Alan Sillitoe's story *The Ragman's Daughter*, will recognise Bulwell as the movie's location. One building which does stand out is **Strelley House**, which dates from 1667 and was founded as a free school by George Strelley. The first governor of the school was William Byron (later 3rd Lord Byron) and, at first, the intake was limited to 30 boys. Above the porch can be seen a carved stone panel which contains the Strelley coat of arms.

Beeston

Lying on the southwest outskirts of Nottingham, Beeston is famous as the home of Boots the Chemist, the pharmaceutical company. Jesse Boot, born in 1850, left school in 1863 to work in his mother's herbalist shop in the centre of Nottingham. The business was started as a sideline to supplement the farm labourer's wages which Jesse's father earned but, following his death when Jesse was only 10 years old, the shop became the mainstay of the family. Buying in bulk in order to offer his customers a discount, Jesse quickly learnt the trade and, with a growing knowledge and interest in drugs, he set up the Boots Pure Drug Company in 1888. The name was chosen to allay customers fears that he was selling adulterated preparations during a price war which he started locally.

The company prospered, largely due to Jesse's business acumen, and by 1896 they had a chain of over 60 shops. Chiefly concentrating on the drugs and preparations side of the business it was at his wife's suggestion that Jesse expanded the lines in the shops to include jewellery, stationary, books, and art. In 1920 the business was sold to an American company only to be bought back by Jesse's son during the depression in 1933. A great benefactor to the city and surrounding area, Jesse was knighted in 1903, created a baronet in 1917, and finally raised to the peerage in 1929, two years before his death.

Beeston is, essentially, an industrial town and, as well as being home to the Boots factory, it was also home to the Humber bicycle factory from 1880. At first employing only 80 staff by 1900 the workforce had risen to 1800; Humber moved into the manufacture of, first, motorcycles and then motorcars in 1903. The company moved its manufacturing base to Coventry in 1908 but the early Humber trademark can still be seen on the old factory building.

Those interested in industrial architecture will find much here to investigate. The ***Anglo-Scotian Mills*** were built in the 1870s by Frank Wilkinson, a major manufacturer of lace although he also had a side line in Shetland wool hosiery. The mill's fanciful façade, however, dates from 1892 when it was built following a severe fire. Close by lies an old silk mill, partly hidden behind the modern shop front windows. Built in 1826 it was burnt to the ground only five years later by rioters. The town's success as an industrial base centres around its communications: the railway and the Beeston Canal. The rather odd looking cottage-style station built by the Midland Railway in 1847 can still be seen as can the lock cottages built for the canal employees in the late 18th century.

The magnificent ***Boat and Horses*** inn stands near to Beeston weir, between Long Eaton and Nottingham, and has been run by Carol Young for the past 15 years. The building dates back to the 18th century and it was here that, in times gone by, the horses from the horse drawn barges that travelled along the River Trent were either changed, rested, or reshod. The inside of this traditional inn is a true picture, with wooden floors and a large selection of interesting memorabilia and trinkets for all to admire. Food is available every lunchtime from a good and varied choice, including some very

The Boat and Horses

popular house daily specials such as home-made chicken curry and chilli con carne. The real ales are kept in excellent condition and range from Theakstons XB to Marstons Pedigree, with a good range of lagers and stouts. There is always something going on at The Boat and Horses, with darts teams, dominoes, a 1960s and 1970s disco on Wednesday and Friday nights and occasional live music at weekends. There is also a safe children's play area within the beer garden and a function room plus large car park for its many visitors. *The Boat and Horses, Trent Road, Beeston, Nottinghamshire NG9 1LP Tel: 0115 925 8589*

South and West of Beeston

Stapleford   Map 3 ref B7
2 miles W of Beeston off A52

In Stapleford churchyard can be found the best preserved Saxon carving in the county in the form of a 10 foot high cross shaft. Dating from the late 11th century, the intricate carving depicts an eagle standing on a serpent, which is said to be the symbol for St Luke. The church, which dates mainly from the 13th and 14th centuries, has many war memorials to its lost heroes. The village was once a thriving centre for framework knitting and terraced cottages built specifically for the workers can still be seen in Nottingham Road.

One other feature of Stapleford which is worthy of a look in **The Hemlockstone**, a massive redstone boulder standing 30 feet high and situated opposite Bramcote Park. It has come to be associated with the Devil, who apparently threw the rock at Lenton Priory whilst in a bad mood and missed. Despite the inaccuracy of aim, the rock was probably deposited here by glacial action, whilst wind erosion has contributed to its brooding appearance. Its geological make up consists of sandstone cemented by the mineral barite, which is found in large quantities throughout the Stapleford and Bramcote Hills. The origins of its name are Celtic and it simply means the stone in the border enclosure.

The village school was renamed the Arthur Mee Centre in memory of the writer who grew up in the town and was educated at the school. Born in 1875, Mee left school at 14 to work for the Nottingham Evening Post before moving to London and finding his niche writing for children. His works include *The Children's Bible* and *The Children's Shakespeare* but it is probably for *The King's England*, a series of guidebooks which ran to some 80 volumes, that Mee is best remembered.

Chilwell
Map 3 ref B7

1 miles S of Beeston on A6005

Although **Chilwell Meadow** only covers some 2 1/2 acres it is important as it is one of the few wet meadows still remaining in the River Trent valley. Several notable wetland plants can be found here including marsh arrow grass and the common spotted orchid.

One of the best places to eat in the area is **The Corn Mill**, an impressive restaurant and inn which was constructed in 1993 on the site of a 19th-century flour mill. A member of the acclaimed Hardys and Hansons Group, The Corn Mill has an attractive red-brick exterior and an interior which successfully captures the atmosphere of days gone by. Stylishly furnished and decorated throughout, the surroundings are enhanced by exposed brick walls and the careful positioning of unusual historic artefacts and memorabilia. Renowned for its food, The Corn Mill offers an extensive selection of home-cooked meals all day, every day. The menu includes a wide variety of starters, snacks, and main courses, including fish, steaks, chicken, and Continental specialities. There is also a good selection of vegetarian dishes as well as with a range daily specials on the chalkboard. Younger diners are very welcome, and there is an excellent value children's menu featuring all the usual favourites. A traditional roast lunch is served on Sundays and a

The Corn Mill

selection of carefully chosen wines, Kimberley ales, and guest beers is available at all times. *The Corn Mill, Swiney Way, Chilwell, Nottinghamshire NG9 6GX Tel: 0115 946 2913*

Toton   Map 3 ref B7
2 miles SW of Beeston on B6003

Lying close to the county border with Derbyshire and in the Erewash Valley, Toton is now, almost exclusively, a quiet, residential area.

The Manor

One of Tom Cobleigh's excellent establishments, *The Manor* began life as a corner café during the early part of the 20th century. It was subsequently converted into an hotel before becoming a public house. Bought by the brewery three years ago, The Manor underwent radical refurbishment and, today, is a very well presented, popular calling point for many customers and families. The decorations and furnishings are first class and there is plenty of interesting memorabilia to admire.

The menu is sure to tantalise even the most jaded palate with dishes such as chicken Tobago, West Country pork, vegetable balti, and brie and broccoli pithivier. The selection is interesting and extensive. General facilities are very good as are those for families and the less abled. The Manor is situated on the main road between Long Eaton and Nottingham. *The Manor, 350 Nottingham Road, Toton, Nottinghamshire NG9 6EF Tel: 0115 946 3266*

Attenborough   *Map 3 ref B7*
1 miles SE of Beeston off the A6005

This compact village has strong links with Oliver Cromwell and the Parliamentarian cause of the 17th century. In 1611, Henry Ireton was born at Ireton House and he went on to become one of the most senior officers in the Parliamentarian army. Fighting at Edgehill and Naseby and also taking part in the siege of Bristol, in 1646 he married Bridget, Cromwell's daughter. Following his military successes and being known for his thoughtful nature, Ireton was appointed as one of the judges who tried and sentenced Charles I. Remaining loyal to Cromwell, he followed his leader to Ireland in 1651 where he died of swamp fever and was buried in Westminster Abbey. However, after the Restoration in 1660, his body, along with that of Cromwell was taken to the gallows at Tyburn where it was put on public display before being beheaded and then buried beneath the gallows. The christening records of Cromwell's granddaughter, Ireton's daughter, can be seen in the village church.

Barton-in-Fabis   *Map 3 ref B7*
2 miles S of Beeston off A453

The village of Barton-in-Fabis (or Barton-in-the-Beans) was once the scene of some anticlimax, if the writings of Sir Osbert Sitwell are to be believed! He described the village in his book *Tales My Father Taught Me*, an account of a retrospective tour made by Sitwell with his father and brother, and apparently it rained solidly during their visit whilst several buildings that he hoped to see had been demolished.

For some 200 years or so, in the 16th and 17th centuries, the manor at Barton was held by the Sacheverells family. Little, however, remains of the grand manor house, which is now incorporated into a farm house, though the brick dovecote is still standing. Built in 1677 for William Sacheverell, this is the only octagonal dovecote in the county and half of the 1,200 nesting boxes survive to this day.

Thrumpton
Map 3 ref B8

3 miles S of Beeston off A453

This quiet village lies right on the border with Derbyshire and, though it has seen many changes, including the building of new houses for those who wish to work in nearby Nottingham and Derby, there is still a village spirit here. Originally called Turmodeston, the small settlement once lay inside the present park of ***Thrumpton Hall***. In the 17th century, John Emerton enclosed the park and new cottages were built for the villagers around the church where some can still be seen today. The H-shaped hall, with Flemish gables, has inside such wonders as a balustrade carved with acanthus scrolls, richly carved doors, and some fine wall panelling dating back to the days of Charles II. The 8th Lord Byron inherited the house through marriage and some relics of the poet Byron are displayed here.

During the 19th century, Lucy, Lady Byron, lived at the hall and it was thanks to her that the village choir was much in demand. She insisted that all her staff have good voices and the choir often sang at Southwell Minster. Lady Byron was also responsible for the restoration of the village church though the old font can now be seen in the churchyard.

Clifton
Map 3 ref B7

2 miles SE of Beeston on A453

At first sight this village near the River Trent seems swamped by modern development but the character of the old village can be found in and around the green. The manor of Clifton was held by the family of that name from the 13th century and, in 1953, they gave up the hall to what is now Nottingham Trent University.

Along the banks of the River Trent is ***Clifton Grove***, a wooded cliff above the riverbank, where visitors can stroll in the footsteps of Paul Morel and Clare Dawes, characters in DH Lawrence's *Sons and Lovers*. This stretch of the River Trent was also the setting for a tragic love story. In 1471, a young squire called Henry Bateman went to the Crusades with his master. When he returned, he discovered that his sweetheart Margaret had fallen for another man and married him. The heart broken lover threw himself into the Trent from Clifton Grove. Some time later, Margaret herself took the same way out, presumably in remorse for her sin.

Ruddington

This historic village, whose name is derived from the Saxon word Rudda - meaning headman - was once the home of many hosiery workers and several of their cottages still remain here. In 1829, a factory and frameworkers cottages were built around a courtyard in Chapel Street. This group of buildings now houses the *Framework Knitters' Museum* and shows the living and working conditions for the workers of the trade. Of the 25 hand frames seen here today, most are fully operational and there is an opportunity to buy samples made at the museum.

The industry reached its height in 1880, with the staggering number of 20,000 frames operating in Nottingham, Derbyshire, and Lincolnshire. As well as the knitting frames on show, the museum also has other machinery of specific importance to the village and the hosiery industry and regular demonstrations are given using the working exhibits.

Not far away is the *Ruddington Village Museum*, housed in the old village school building of 1852. Concentrating on the everyday life of the villagers there are reconstructions of several shops and craftsmen's workshops including an Edwardian fish and chip shop. As well as having one of the school rooms restored to look as it once did, there is also a room devoted to a collection of farming implements.

South of Ruddington

Gotham   *Map 3 ref B8*
3 miles SW of Ruddington off A453

The name is actually pronounced Goat'm and the village should not be confused with the home of the caped crusader, Batman. However, the village is remembered as the home of the Wise Men. King John had decreed that he wished to build a hunting lodge here in the village. Naturally displeased at having to give up their land to the king's whims, the villagers devised a plan. They decided that the best way to dissuade the royal presence was to feign madness. When the king's messengers entered the village, the inhabitants reacted in such a peculiar way that the men returned to His Majesty with the suggestion that the mad men of Gotham should be left well alone. Such were the odd tales of their bizarre acts that Dr Andrew Borde published the *Merrie Tales of the Mad Men of Gotham* in the 16th century. There are many bizarre stories but one of the finest is kept alive in the name of the village pub - The Cuckoo

Bush. A group of villagers, captivated by the song of a cuckoo, decided to capture the bird by encircling the bush in which it was sitting by a fence. Unfortunately, the men did not think to build a roof so the cuckoo simply flew away to escape imprisonment.

Ratcliffe on Soar
Map 3 ref B8

6 miles SE of Ruddington off A453

The tiny village of Ratcliffe on Soar has a pretty little church, with an eye-catching blackened spire, and a handsome manor farmhouse set picturesquely on the meadow banks of the River Soar. Although a massive power station looms over everything and the railway clatters by, this charming village is still definitely worth a visit.

Holy Trinity Church, with its broach spire and four pinnacles, houses the splendid tombs belonging to the Sacheverells. A Ralph, three Henrys, and their wives lie here under the watchful gaze of the cooling towers. Here too, Sir Osbert found fault with his ancestors' resting places, having apparently discovered the church under water when he came to pay his last respects!

West Leake
Map 3 ref B8

5 miles S of Ruddington off the A6006

Recorded in the Domesday Book as Leche, this surprisingly rural village has two Roman tracks on its boundaries as well as evidence of Roman occupation. The remains of the fishpools which stood near the medieval manor house can still be made out though the house ceased to be the home of the lord of the manor in 1750.

East Leake
Map 3 ref B8

4 miles S of Ruddington off the A60

Like its neighbour, West Leake, the village name is derived from the Anglo-Saxon word Leche, meaning water meadow, and both villages lie on the banks of a tributary of the River Soar. The village church, which was mentioned in the Domesday Survey of 1086, was extensively restored in the 19th century but it has retained its prize possession, a **Vamp Horn**. Some 8 feet long and known in the village as the Shawm, only five other churches are known to have such an instrument. Invented in 1670 by Samuel Morland, the horn was used by the bass singer to lead the choir from the gallery.

Sutton Bonington
Map 3 ref B8

6 miles SW of Ruddington off A6006

On the banks of the River Soar, the village has some lovely buildings, including its two churches, and it is also home to the Nottingham University School of Agriculture. The village too was the site of an ancient settlement and excavations have revealed a pagan Anglo-Saxon cemetery here. Originally two hamlets, both the churches, St Michael's of Bonnington and St Anne's of Sutton, date from the 13th century. However, one of the finest buildings in the village is the hall, which was built in the 18th century by Beaumont Parkyns, the brother of the Wrestling Baronet of Bunny.

Normanton on Soar
Map 3 ref B8
7 miles SW of Ruddington off A6006

Lying in the valley of the River Soar, which at this point marks the county boundary with Leicestershire, the village is centred around its charming, early 13th-century *St James' Church*. Fortunately the building has been completely restored following a devastating fire in 1986 and its tall, broached spire, considered the best example in England, has been returned to is former glory.

Standford on Soar
Map 3 ref B8
7 miles S of Ruddington off A6006

At the southernmost point of Nottinghamshire, it is at Standford on Soar that the River Soar, the King's Brook, and the Grand Union Canal make their individual paths across the county. Here also lie the disused railway lines of the Great Central Railway that once stretched from Nottingham to Marylebone. The church interior has some lovely decorative stencilling and many monuments to the Dashwood family. Stanford Hall, which was built in 1771, is now a Co-operative College, and from here the wonderful views of Charnwood Forest can be enjoyed.

Widmerpool
Map 3 ref C8
5 miles SE of Ruddington off the A606

This village is widely regarded as one of Nottinghamshire's oldest settlements and it is believed to have been in existence in the days of the Romans. In its history, the village has seen many changes and, an estate village from 1283, the ownership of the land has been disputed several times. Widmerpool was also embroiled in the Civil War with the battle of Willoughby Fields taking place close by.

The new Widmerpool Hall, which is now an AA training centre, was built by the Robinson family who came to the village from Scotland in the early 19th century. At this time too, the village church was greatly in need of repair, which was made worse by a lightning strike in 1836. The family not only restored the church but did much building work in the village and much of Widmerpool seen today it their handiwork.

Willoughby-on-the-Wolds
Map 3 ref C8
6 miles SE of Ruddington off A46

Lying close to the county border with Leicestershire it is not uncommon to see the huntsmen of the Quorn riding through the parish. The Quorn Hunt also meets in the village several times in the season and they are often joined by Prince Charles.

This is an ancient village, its name being derived from the Danish word Wilgebi - meaning village of the willows. Close by lies the Roman road, Fosse Way, and a Roman settlement, **Vernemetum**, has been found near to the site of an Anglo-Saxon burial ground.

Stanton on the Wolds
Map 3 ref C8
4 miles SE of Ruddington off A606

This rural village, which was until the 1960s home to seven dairy farms, has few really old buildings though the village dates back to Norman times. In the late 18th century, Stanton was hit by a freak storm in which giant hailstones rained down on the cottages and smashed their roofs. The ancient village **Church of All Saints** did, however, survive and it can be found standing alone in a field and reached by a footpath. Dating from the 11th century, the church, one of the smallest in south Nottinghamshire, is built mostly of boulders some of which, undoubtedly, came from nearby Fosse Way.

Keyworth
Map 3 ref C8
3 miles E of Ruddington off A606

In the heart of south Nottinghamshire's farming country this, until very recently, small village prides itself in producing no less than 30 professional cricketers, one of which went on to be capped for England. The village too has had its share of scandals and one local legend tells of a tenant farmer who was visited by the rector who had a complaint to discuss. The farmer was not very agreeable to the criticism and soundly horse whipped the clergyman before sending him on his way. This whip is still in existence though the nature of the complaint the rector was making is unknown.

Plumtree
Map 3 ref C7
2 miles E of Ruddington off the A606

This old, former agricultural village has seen many of its farms, and those families who worked the land, disappear and the remaining two farms which formed the Burnside estate were purchased by the Duchy of Cornwall in 1988. Plumtree also had a working windmill, situated on a hilltop, that was owned, in the early 20th century, by a local magistrate. One day, in court, the magistrate, who was also a publican, found before him two gentlemen called for being drunk and disorderly. The magistrate imposed fines upon the men and, a week later, his windmill was burnt to the ground. Whether this was an accident or an act of revenge was never discovered.

Bunny
Map 3 ref C7

2 miles S of Ruddington on A60

This pretty village has a wealth of lovely architecture and owes much of its charm to the eccentricities of its former 18th-century squire, Sir Thomas Parkyns. A man obsessed with the sport of wrestling, he employed two full time professionals to spar with him at Bunny Hall. He also organised an annual tournament in the village to promote local wrestling talent and this event continued nearly 70 years after its originator's death. In St Mary's Church, which was designed by Sir Thomas, his memorial graphically illustrates his commitment to the sport. It depicts the squire standing victorious over his defeated opponent on a wrestling mat, while Old Father Time stands by, perhaps as referee.

The village has some ancient woodland, **Bunny Wood**, which was mentioned in the Domesday Book. Consisting mainly of elm, oak, and ash, the woodland is also home to over 30 species of birds and it is managed by the Nottinghamshire Wildlife Trust.

CHAPTER TWO
Newark-on-Trent and the Vale of Belvoir

Norman doorway, St Giles' Church,
Balderton

Chapter 2 - Area Covered

*For precise location of places please refer to the colour
maps found at the rear of the book.*

● East Retford

● Worksop

● Mansfield
Woodhouse

● Mansfield

NOTTINGHAMSHIRE

● Sutton in Ashfield

Newark
on Trent ●

● Kirkby in Ashfield

● Hucknall

● Arnold

● NOTTINGHAM

● Beeston

2
Newark-on-Trent and the Vale of Belvoir

Introduction

This southeastern area of the county, south of the great Roman road, Fosse Way (now known as the A46), is a mass of small rural villages and hamlets. In the south, bordering the county of Leicestershire, these ancient settlements overlook the Vale of Belvoir and it was here that Thomas Cranmer, in the village of Aslockton, spent his early years.

Further north, on the banks of the River Trent and also near to the county border with Lincolnshire, lies the historic town of Newark-on-Trent. The key market town for this area of Nottinghamshire, Newark prospered due to its position, on the Fosse Way and Great North Road, as well as being able to take advantage of the river. A medieval wool town, it is the stories of the Civil War and the sieges that the townsfolk had to endure which captures the imagination of visitors today.

In fact, there are few places in southeast Nottinghamshire which did not escape the ravages of this bitter struggle between king and Parliament in the mid-17th century. With Newark a Royalist stronghold and the local gentry on the side of Cromwell, though no major battles were fought on Nottinghamshire soil, there were many skirmishes and here, as elsewhere, country houses and other buildings were destroyed by both sides.

One battle, however, did take place here, in 1487, during the War of the Roses when the army of Henry VII defeated the House of York at East Stoke in a particularly bloody engagement.

Bingham

An old medieval market town which grew up around the church, Bingham, after going through a period of depression in the 19th century, is once again thriving. Most of the buildings around the market place are Victorian, including the Butter Cross. All Saints' Church, however, is medieval, dating from the 13th century though, again, there are many Victorian additions and decorations.

George Abbot, a vicar from Bingham who went on to become the Archbishop of Canterbury, had an uneventful reign except for one unfortunate accident in 1621. He was out shooting deer with a crossbow when he missed and killed a gamekeeper instead.

South and West of Bingham

Radcliffe on Trent   *Map 4 ref C7*
3 miles W of Bingham on the A52

Once an estate village for nearby Holme Pierrepoint, Radcliffe on Trent grew up around a Roman crossing over the river and a Saxon manor was also founded here.

Ashmores Restaurant, in the heart of Radcliffe on Trent, is very much a family run establishment: brothers Mark and Max are the very experienced chefs and they are ably assisted by their wives Jo and Emma. Mum and Dad, Gill and Clive, are also on hand to help out. Though the family have only been here for a year or so, they have established an enviable reputation not only for their excellent cuisine but also for the cosy and intimate atmosphere of the restaurant.

Ashmores Restaurant

The menu here is very French in style but with a difference that is all the brothers' own. There is always an excellent and interesting choice to be made and the menu itself changes every three months. As the tables in the restaurant are booked for the evening, there is ample opportunity for diners to enjoy their meal in comfort and without haste. Everything is freshly prepared to order, except for the breads, ice creams, and sorbets, and as well as being a delight to eat the presentation is a sight to behold.

The interior decor too adds much to the relaxing and friendly ambience of Ashmores Restaurant. Spacious and airy, the walls display a range of pictures and prints by local and not so local artists, all of which are for sale. To add to the intimacy, the tables are well spaced and, around the room, potted flowers and shrubs created discreet partitions between the parties. Ashmores Restaurant is open between 12.00 and 14.00 from Tuesday to Saturday and, as well as serving light lunches and snacks there is also a reasonably priced set four course lunch. On Sundays a set priced three course traditional lunch is served. *Ashmores Restaurant, 1 Bingham Road, Radcliffe on Trent, Nottinghamshire NG12 2FY Tel: 0115 933 2001*

Thornton's Holt caravan and camping park is set within 14 acres of attractive pasture land just south of Radcliffe on Trent and with some very pleasant hamlets and villages nearby. The ideal place for a holiday base, Anne and Philip Taylor, the charming owners, have gone very much out of their way to ensure than all who

Thornton's Holt Camping Park

stay here have a wonderful holiday. The park's user's guide is packed full of information from interesting and exciting places to visit down to practical details and the restaurant listings. Their reception area is also as informative as a tourist information centre, if not more so, and the couple are always happy to offer help, advice and directions to ensure that all holidaymakers get the most out of their stay in the area.

The facilities of the site itself are excellent. Apart from the practical amenities there is also plenty here for children including the heated indoor swimming pool and the extensive, safe play area, with the famous Stragglethorpe death slide. Well mannered dogs are welcome and there are also facilities for equestrian pursuits. *Thornton's Holt Camping Park, Stragglethorpe, Radcliffe on Trent, Nottinghamshire NG12 2JZ Tel: 0115 933 2125*

Cotgrave   Map 4 ref C7
4 miles SW of Bingham off the A46
The discovery of an Anglo-Saxon burial ground on **Mill Hill**, Cotgrave's highest point, confirms that there has been a settlement here for many centuries. The excavation team uncovered the skeletons of nearly 100 people including some 13 children and the remains have been dated to around the mid to late 6th century.

Close to the burial ground stood the village's old post mill, itself the site of an unsolved mystery. One of the millers disappeared without trace after having been accused of pilfering corn. Rumours in the 19th century suggested that a body had been discovered in the mill foundations and, despite believing that this could be the remains of the missing miller, the villagers kept quiet and the rumour was never investigated. During an excavation of the post mill site in the 1970s the skeleton of a male was uncovered which showed injuries that suggested that the unfortunate man was killed by a blow to the head. Whether or not this was all that remained of the missing miller has never been established.

However, Cotgrave is probably most well known as the home of Cotgrave Colliery which opened in 1963 and was a showplace mine for a number of years. The promise of work here for the next 100 years brought many miners from other coalfields to the village and also a huge expansion and building programme. The optimism of the 1960s did not last and, by the end of the 1980s, the colliery had all but shut down due to major geological faults.

Kinoulton   Map 3 ref C8
6 miles S of Bingham off the A46
The village, on the edge of the wolds, stands on high ground and from this vantage point there are views over the Vale of Belvoir to Belvoir Castle. Today, Kinoulton is a large commuter village but it

has a long and interesting past which is easily overlooked. In the 12th century, Kinoulton was the site of a castle, its commanding position being ideal and it also lay close to the Fosse Way. Cranmer was thought to have had a palace here and, to the west of the village, lies the spring which brought the village to prominence in Georgian times as a spa with curative properties.

Dominating the northern edge of the village is an avenue of poplars which lead up to Vimy Ridge Farm. Planted by Sir Jesse Hind, whose son was killed at Vimy, France during World War I, the 188 trees are said to represent the officers who fell in battle with his son. The farm, once a busy, bustling place, now lies in ruins and the huts which Sir Jesse hired to housed ex-servicemen during the Depression of the 1930s are ruined and overgrown.

Hickling   *Map 4 ref C8*
7 miles S of Bingham off the A606
Lying on the western edge of the Vale of Belvoir, this agricultural village was also the site of a busy basin on the Grantham Canal. Building work on the basin finished in 1797 and the canal, which carried coal, building materials, and agricultural goods, was in constant used until the 1930s when it began to fall into disuse. Recently cleared, **Hickling Basin** is once again attracting people, this time visitors who come to see the resident flocks of wildfowl.

Upper Broughton   *Map 3 ref C8*
9 miles S of Bingham on the A606
The site of a Roman settlement, the village was once called Broughton Sulney, though this name is now only used for ecclesiastical purposes. This alternative name stems from Norman times when the village and surrounding land was owned by Aluredus de Sulnei.

In the centre of the village are its two greens, the first of which, in springtime, is a riot of golden daffodils that includes the species named Upper Broughton. On the second green can be seen the remains of a cross which is thought to have been placed here to commemorate the end of the Black Plague in Upper Broughton.

Colston Bassett   *Map 4 ref D7*
4 miles S of Bingham off the A46
This small village was, at one time, large enough to hold a weekly market and, although Colston Bassett has considerably diminished in size, the partly medieval Market Cross can still be seen near the old post office. Owned by the National Trust, it was their first prop-

erty in Nottinghamshire. The land around the village, which lies on the county border with Leicestershire, has been farmed by several great families over the years. From the time of Henry I the manor was owned by the Bassett family and the village was so named to distinguish it from Drayton Bassett in Staffordshire.

During the time of the Civil War in the 17th century, Manor Farm was the home of the Hacker family who claimed to have two brothers living under the same roof but with their loyalties lying in opposing camps. Francis Hacker was the only member of the family to support the Parliamentarians and, a fine soldier and militia commander, he was given the task of warder to Charles I. Responsible for the king whilst he was in London, Francis also had to ensure that Charles I was executed on 30th January. Francis Hacker remained loyal to Cromwell during the years of the Commonwealth, becoming a Member of Parliament for Leicester, but, after the Restoration, Hacker was arrested and eventually executed on the gallows at Tyburn.

Cropwell Bishop   Map 3 ref C7
3 miles SW of Bingham off the A46
The oldest building in this compact village is St Giles' Church which dates back to 1215. Close to the old and still used Roman road, Fosse Way, the coaching inns of Cropwell Bishop are said to have given shelter to highwayman Dick Turpin whilst he was plundering the coaches using the busy road.

Cropwell Butler   Map 3 ref C7
2 miles SW of Bingham off the A46
Mentioned in the Domesday Book, Cropwell Butler is often twinned with its neighbour, Tithby, and it is here that the parish Church of Holy Trinity can be found. A quiet and rural place, the village does, however, have one famous son, Thomas Smith. Born in 1621, Thomas, the son of a small landowner in Cropwell Butler, went on the found a group of banks which are now part of National Westminster. The NatWest branch in South Parade, Nottingham is still referred to as Smith's Bank Branch.

South and East of Bingham

Langar   Map 4 ref D7
3 miles S of Bingham off the A52
This small village lies on an escarpment which slopes down to the River Strome and it was the Saxons, calling the area The Lang Ridge,

which gave the village its name. The village **Church of St Andrew** dates from the 13th century though it was heavily restored in the 1860s by the incumbent rector, Thomas Butler, father of the novelist Samuel Butler. However, several ancient monuments remain inside including a memorial to Admiral Lord Howe, a descendent of the Scroope family. He led the British to defeat against the French in the Battle of the Glorious 1st of June and, from then on, he became known as Black Dick of Langar.

The old village rectory, now privately owned, is a very attractive Queen Anne building and it as here, in 1835, that Samuel Butler was born. By all accounts his childhood was an unhappy one and, after finishing his education at St John's College, Cambridge, Samuel travelled to New Zealand. Following his success in the sheep rearing business, Samuel returned to London, England where he continued his writing and began to paint. His first novel, based on his experiences in New Zealand was published in 1872 and this was followed by further novels before he turned his attention to nonfiction and, in particular, the theories of Charles Darwin.

Also in Langar is the **Wild Flower Farm Visitors Centre**, part of a commercial nursery, where visitors are able to explore the wild flower meadows and see a wide variety of species in their natural habitat.

Granby   *Map 4 ref D7*
4 miles SE of Bingham off the A52

This small, once self-sufficient village is still proud that it gave its name and the title of Marquis to the Duke of Rutland whose family had purchased the estate. As Colonel-in-Chief of the British Army, John, the eldest son of the 3rd Duke of Rutland, was immensely popular with his troops and his successful career was marked by the granting of the title the Marquis of Granby. Naturally enough, the village pub bears the name The Marquis of Granby!

Sutton   *Map 4 ref D7*
4 miles E of Bingham off the A52

This little hamlet, which is sometimes called Sutton-cum-Granby, has been in existence for over 1000 years and it still remains remarkably unspoilt. Situated in the Vale of Belvoir and overshadowed by Belvoir Castle, Sutton once had its own **Castle**. This was not a grand stone affair but rather a fortified homestead with a moat to which villagers could retire and seek shelter in troubled times. Traces of the moat can still be seen in the fields. Though the fortified house no longer exists, Sutton is home to one of the smallest chapels in the country. Measuring just 18 feet square and with its door opening straight onto the village's main street **Sutton Chapel** was built in 1860. The organ was installed in the 1920s and, until then, hymns were either sung unaccompanied or with the help of a loaned harmonium, though the owner insisted that the instrument not be left in the chapel between services.

Whatton

Map 4 ref D7

3 miles E of Bingham off the A52

The Norman **St John's Church** was restored in the 1860s under the direction of Thomas Butler, rector of Langar, and the stained glass windows, including some to the designs of Burne-Jones, were added in the late 19th century. The font, which is dated 1662, replaced the one that had been damaged during the Commonwealth. This church was used by Thomas Cranmer up until he left the area to take up his studies at Cambridge. A memorial to his father, Thomas Cranmer senior, who died in 1501, can be found inside.

Aslockton

Map 4 ref D7

2 miles E of Bingham off the A52

This village is now separated from its neighbour, Whatton, by the main Nottingham to Grantham railway line, though the footpaths linking the two can still be walked today. This was the village in which Thomas Cranmer was born and spent his early years. Born in 1489, he attended the parish church at Whatton and also a local grammar school, possibly at Southwell, before, at the age of 14, continuing his education at Cambridge. An obscure theologian and academic, it was in 1533 that Henry VIII selected Cranmer as the Archbishop of Canterbury. He was also the last archbishop to be appointed by Rome, with the approval of the king.

One of Cranmer's first duties on gaining his appointment was to pronounce the marriage between Henry VIII and Catherine of Aragon null and void; throughout his 23 years in office, Cranmer also pronounced invalid Henry's marriage to Anne Boleyn and granted him a divorce from Anne of Cleeves. Loyal to his monarch throughout, Cranmer aided Henry in effecting the break of the Church in England from Rome. He was also responsible for drafting much of the Common Prayer book that was used right up until the 1970s when a modern language version was published. Following the death of Henry VIII, Cranmer was convicted of treason by Mary I and burnt at the stake in 1556.

Though not built until the late 19th century, Aslockton **Church** is appropriately dedicated to St Thomas whilst the village school also bears the name of its most famous resident. ***Cranmer's Mound***, to the east of the church, is a high Norman motte of some 15 feet which is clearly visible from the footpath to Orston. Further along this same footpath can be seen the site of the manor house where Cranmer was born.

Newark-on-Trent

Historically, Newark-on-Trent has always been a strategic point: it lies close to the Roman road, Fosse Way, and also guards the first upstream crossing of the River Trent. Though there is no evidence of a Roman settlement here, the remains of pottery and coins found in the vicinity of the castle suggest that there was possibly a fort here at one time. The Saxons certainly settled here and part of their defences for the town have been excavated. It was, however, the Danes who began the formation of Newark-on-Trent as it is known today. The evidence of their occupation is particularly obvious in the use of gate (from the Danish gata meaning street) in the names of the many roads - Castle Gate, Balderton Gate, and Barnby Gate.

Newark Castle

By the time of the Domesday Survey, the name Newark, a corruption of New Work, was being used. This name was either used to refer to the rebuilding of the town following the Danish invasion or it could have been a reference to the new town defences that were constructed around that time. Occupying a strong defensive position beside the River Trent, ***Newark Castle*** did not serve a particular military service. Built in the 12th century, it is not known for certain which parts of the castle are the oldest and there may have been a former wooden structure on this site prior to the great stone building still seen today. However, it is known that the castle was founded by Alexander, Bishop of Lincoln. Over the next 300 years, the castle saw extensive improvements made to its original construction and, in 1483, it was taken from the bishops of Lincoln by Henry VII, who leased it to a succession of noblemen until the time of the Civil War.

Throughout the bitter Civil War, Newark remained staunchly loyal to the Crown and, along with the castle, it withstood several sieges. By the end of the war, Newark-on-Trent was in a terrible state as not only had little food and other supplies been able to reach the besieged town but the plague had broken out. The victorious Parliamentarians quickly ordered the destruction of the castle and though their orders were carried out by the local residents, the townsfolk were in such a depleted state that the task was never completed. The gutted remains can still be seen, as a prominent landmark in the town, but they are not the only reminder to the present day visitor of the town's valiant efforts to withstand bombardment by Cromwell's army.

In order to ensure that Newark had suitable defences to withstand attack, two small forts were built to guard this strategic crossing over the River Trent. (The only other crossing, at Nottingham, was held by the Parliamentarians.) The King's Sconce, to the northeast, has since disappeared but its twin, **Queen's Sconce** still lies to the southeast. Named after Queen Henrietta Maria, who brought supplies into the town after the first siege in 1643, this square earthwork had a bastion in each corner and a hollow in the middle.

There are other reminders of the Civil War in Newark-on-Trent and, in the middle of the town, on Kirk Gate, are **Henrietta Maria's Lodgings**, where, legend has it, the queen stayed on her visit to the town in 1643. Travelling from Bridlington to the king's headquarters at Oxford, the queen was carrying with her men and arms from the continent which she had paid for by selling some of the Crown Jewels. On one side of the market square lies the White Hart inn, where soldiers where billeted. At the time of Charles I's last visit to the town, the landlord, Gilbert Atkinson, asked for and was granted safe passage by Parliament to quit Newark-on-Trent and move to Nottingham. Sick and elderly, Gilbert took with him his son Thomas and, years later, when Thomas returned such was the resentment at his desertion that Thomas Atkinson's bust in the church was damaged by the angry townsfolk.

Close by the inn can be found **The Governor's House**; the place where the governors of Newark lived during the Civil War and also the place where Charles I quarrelled with Prince Rupert after the prince had lost Bristol to Parliament. This wonderful timber framed building was restored in the late 19th century and during the work a medieval wall and some beam paintings were revealed along with some graffiti dating from 1757.

Also found in the heart of Newark-on-Trent is Nottinghamshire's finest parish church; its fine spire dominating the town and acting as a local landmark. The **Church of St Mary Magdalen** dates back to the early 12th century though all that survives of that structure is the crypt which now houses the treasury. Much of the building seen today dates from the 14th, 15th, and 16th centuries and its exterior is a fascinating blend of carvings and tracery.

A walk around this charming town will reveal all manner of delightful and ancient buildings and two of the major banks provide marvellous examples of Victorian banking decor. One of these, the National Westminster, on the corner of Stodman Street, was built on the site of a house owned by an alderman during the Civil War. With Newark-on-Trent under siege, the alderman's dreams were disturbed several times by visions of the house burning down. Not one to ignore bad omens, he packed up his family and possessions and left. Shortly afterwards, cannon fire set the house ablaze.

Situated by the river in Devon Park is **St Catherine's Well**, the origins of which are linked with a sad and tragic legend. During the 13th century, Sir Guy Saucimer killed his friend, Sir Everard Bevorcotes, in a jealous rage after Sir Everard had won the heart of Isabell de Caldwell, whom they both loved. From the place where Sir Everard fell a spring gushed forth and, guilt ridden, Sir Guy travelled abroad. Whilst he was away, Isabell died from grief and Sir Guy caught leprosy. One night, St Catherine appeared in dream to the knight and told him that he would be cured if he returned to Newark and bathed in the spring. Sir Guy travelled back to Nottinghamshire and washed in the well and, as St Catherine had said, he was cured of the illness. After this miracle cure, Sir Guy built a chapel beside the spring and from then on lived a life dedicated to God.

With such a wealth of history inside its boundaries, Newark-on-Trent also has its fair share of museums. **Newark Museum** is housed in a former school which dates back to 1529 and the history of the town is traced from its early beginnings, with exhibitions of prehistoric artefacts and Roman finds, through to the desperate days of the Civil War. A large Anglo-Saxon cemetery, discovered in Millgate, is also on display. At the town hall, the town's fine collection of silverware, including some 99 siege pieces, can be seen in the **Newark Civic Plate Collection**. Planned by the town council, the **Civil War Trail** is a 23 mile walking and driving route which takes in many of the villages and towns between Newark-on-Trent and Nottingham that have links with either side in the bloody dispute. Details of the trail from the tourist information centre.

After the turbulent times of the 17th century, Newark-on-Trent returned to its former life as a quiet town, serving the needs of the surrounding communities. However, its position on the River Trent played an important part in its development during the Industrial Revolution. Goods were transported along the River Trent from Nottingham to the North Sea and a wealth of warehouses grew up along the riverbank. Sadly, commercial water traffic has declined to almost nothing in the second half of the 20th century but one of the old warehouses is now the home of the **Millgate Folk Museum**. Concentrating on everyday life in the 19th and 20th centuries, the museum has an interesting array of shops and shop fronts and there is also a reconstruction of an early 20th-century terraced house.

On the outskirts of the town, at **Beacon Hill**, one of the greatest defeats over the Roundheads took place, in 1644, when Prince Rupert arrived to lift the second of Newark's sieges. Under Sir John Meldrum, the Parliamentarians lost more arms and equipment than during any other engagement of the Civil War. Also just outside the town, close to the A1, lies the **Newark Air Museum**, which has over 30 aircraft on display. Opened in the 1960s, the museum also has a great deal of aviation memorabilia, relics, and uniforms on display. One of the largest privately managed collections in the country, visitors can see jet fighters, bombers, and helicopters which span the history of aviation.

Portland Street Antiques Centre is housed within an impressive building which was once Christ Church School, a boys school dating back some 150 years. Before becoming an antiques centre in the early 1990s, it was also used as a brewery and a warehouse, but many of the old school room features remain. Covering some three floors, this is a real Aladdin's cave for anyone interested in antiques and collectibles. There are over 100 dealers here with all manner of items on show and, with a plenty of space to move around, it is a joy to wander around and view the items. Helpful and knowledgeable staff are on hand to help find a particular item and, in this relaxed and pleasant atmosphere, browsing is positively encouraged.

In the summer of 1997 a further attraction was added to the centre when the ground floor tea room was opened. Well decorated and furnished, this is the ideal place to stop for a snack or light meal

Portland Street Antiques Centre

while wandering round the displays. Newark and the surrounding area is well known for its antiques and every two months an International Antiques Fair is held on the Showground. *Portland Street Antiques Centre, 27-31 Portland Street, Newark-on-Trent, Nottinghamshire NG24 4XF Tel: 01636 74397*

The odd looking ***Swan and Salmon Tap*** public house can be found next to the castle, at the point where the Newark Town Lock meets the River Trent. The building dates from before 1770, when

The Swan and Salmon Tap

it was first mentioned as a stop for post coaches travelling to Edinburgh, Carlisle, York, and Scarborough. Much later, in 1887, the building seen today was built on the Trent frontage with one wall built on top of the river wall. During floods in January 1928, the river wall gave way and part of the building collapsed into the Trent. A considerable part of the pub was closed and the wing extending to the river bank was never rebuilt. This has left a large scar on the building and this is what gives the Swan and Salmon Tap its distinctive look.

In the summer of 1996, owner Malcolm McLean reopened the Swan and Salmon Tap after an extensive refurbishment and since then it has gone from strength to strength. The downstairs bar areas are traditional, with quarry tiled and wooden floors and plenty of memorabilia decorating the walls. Upstairs is The Locker Room sports bar, complete with a pool table and an interesting collection of Rugby shorts that have been worn by well-known players. There is also a big screen TV which shows many of the important league and cup football matches that are only available on satellite television. This is a popular and lively pub, which also serves tasty meals and bar snacks between noon and 15.00 and provides live music each Wednesday evening. *The Swan and Salmon Tap, Swan and Salmon Yard, Castlegate, Newark-on-Trent, Nottinghamshire NG24 1BG Tel: 01636 613340*

Ye Olde Market public house stands opposite the castle on one of the main roads through Newark. Formerly called the Ram Hotel, there has been a building here for over 400 years though the one

Ye Olde Market

seen today is Georgian. Very much at the heart of this old town, the pub opens in the morning to serve coffee and stays open to offer refreshment throughout the day. Pleasantly decorated and furnished, a whole array of articles can be seen hanging from the walls and ceilings, including an old wooden wheelbarrow. The market theme runs throughout the pub and, along with the old pictures and prints of the town, makes an interesting and unusual interior.

In the evenings the mood of the pub changes and this becomes a lively place for the young and young at heart. There is live entertainment in the evenings from Wednesday to Sunday and Ye Olde Market really buzzes. There are also 14 comfortable guest letting rooms available throughout the year. *Ye Olde Market, 19 Castlegate, Newark-on-Trent, Nottinghamshire NG24 1AZ Tel: 01636 702255*

Housed in a late Georgian building on one of the town's main streets is **Gannets Café**, a meeting and eating place for people with taste. Hilary and David opened the café back in 1979 and since then they have gone from strength to strength and Gannets now enjoys an enviable reputation in the surrounding area.

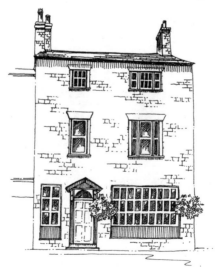

Gannets Café

Well decorated, light and airy inside, there is plenty of room in this no smoking café whilst, during fine weather, there is also a lovely garden patio for patrons to use. Relaxed and informal, there is a mouthwatering choice of delicious freshly prepared and home-cooked dishes which can be ordered from the counter. To encourage guests to linger for longer there is an array to daily newspapers on hand

and Gannets is fully licensed to sell alcohol with meals. For those who are unable to stay and enjoy the food, Gannets has a takeaway service and also a Provisions Shop which sells a range of quality ingredients including local organic flours, olives, and balsamic vinegar. *Gannets Café, 35 Castlegate, Newark-on-Trent, Nottinghamshire NG24 1AZ Tel: 01636 702066*

The White Swan is a charming black and white 17th-century coaching house that is hard to miss. However, what is not so obvious from the outside is the wonderful hospitality offered by Tracey and Ben Vidler, the landlady and landlord. Decorated and furnished in a manner in keeping with the age of the building, there are numerous small alcoves to offer privacy but also plenty of room for everyone. There is a small, separate restaurant area, though meals can be taken anywhere in the pub, and, to the rear, there is a games' room which is as comfortable as the rest of the place.

The White Swan

Though Tracey and Ben have only been at the White Swan for a short time, they have gained an enviable reputation in Newark and the surrounding area for the imaginative and delicious meals and bar snacks on the menu. No fish or chicken with chips here, the resident chef produces a mouthwatering array of freshly prepared dishes which combine tastes from all over the world with a Continental flair. Such is the popularity of the White Swan that it is becoming essential to book a table in the evenings but for those who just enjoy a good pint, there is always an excellent range of hand-pulled ales. *The White Swan, 50 Northgate, Newark-on-Trent, Nottinghamshire NG24 1HF Tel: 01636 704700*

Recently built in rural surroundings, **The Lord Ted** was opened in September 1996 by the now Deputy Prime Minister, John Prescott. He actually pulled the first pint here and it is probably reasonable to suppose that he drank one too. The political connections do not end there as the pub is named after Ted Bishopthorpe, a local Member of Parliament and the last Labour MP to move from the House of Commons to the Lords. As might be expected, one area of this well furnished pub is dedicated to the man and contains all manner of memorabilia. Other themes around the pub contain the more usual pictures and tackle associated with fishing and horses.

The Lord Ted

Though The Lord Ted is relatively new, the overall feel, both inside and out, is of a much older establishment. Along with this goes the old fashioned style of hospitality where customer satisfaction comes first. Open all day, every day, there is a tasty menu which contains many favourites that is supplemented by the daily specials chalkboard. Those interested in beer will be pleased to see the wide range of real ales on tap. This is also very much a family pub and children are especially welcome. They have their own menu and there is a superb, safe outdoor playarea. *The Lord Ted, Farndon Road, Newark-on-Trent, Nottinghamshire NG24 4SW Tel: 01636 612626*

Smeaton's Lakes is a wonderful combination of countryside amenities all within easy reach of the many attractions of the East Midlands. Covering some 80 acres, this attractive site of lakes and parkland offers a quiet haven for caravanners and campers as well as excellent fishing.

The camping amenities are second to none and reflect the high standard of this site which was only opened in 1996. The various lakes are well stocked and will keep both the coarse fisherman and the carp angler happy for many hours. Though Smeaton's Lakes has only been open for a short time it has a long history. English Heritage have dated the site back to the times of the Pilgrim Fathers and an old battery earthwork, which held a cannon during the Civil War, is also here.

Smeaton's Lakes

This area of the county, towards the Lincolnshire border, is flat and constantly under the threat of flooding. Many years ago, a bridge builder, John Smeaton, recognising the threat devised a raised bridge to compensate for the rising water levels. One of his bridges also stands here and he also lends his name to this unusual and unique place. *Smeaton's Lakes, Great North Road, Newark-on-Trent, Nottinghamshire NG23 6ED Tel: 01636 605088/73250*

South of Newark-on-Trent

Balderton   Map 4 ref E5
2 miles SE of Newark-on-Trent on the A1
This rural village has expanded greatly throughout this century and it now has several industries, shops, schools, and housing estates. However, many of the village's original old buildings can still be seen including the toll house which stands as a reminder to the days of stage coach traffic along the Great North Road.
The crooked spire of **St Giles' Church** dominates the main crossroads in the village. The fine, decorated Norman doorway, which dates from the 13th century, is much visited by architects and its plague plaque and numerous memorials to battles, both home and abroad, tell of the events which affected the lives of the villagers.

Alverton   Map 4 ref D6
7 miles S of Newark-on-Trent off the A52
A small hamlet of just a handful of houses, Alverton is also home to two ghosts. The first has been seen in the old Church of England

schoolhouse, which is now a private residence, and it is believed to be the ghost of a teacher who was murdered at the school.

Alverton's second ghost, an elderly lady dressed in Victorian clothes, has been sighted at one of the hamlet's larger houses. The lady is believed to be Mary Brown, a sewing maid to Queen Victoria, who gave up her job after the death of her sister-in-law. Mary moved back to brother's house to act as housekeeper to him and his four children and, by all accounts, she proved to be a formidable woman. Ruling the house with a rod of iron, in later years, when noises were heard on the upper floors, it was said that "Aunt Polly was on the warpath again!"

Orston   Map 4 ref D7
8 miles S of Newark-on-Trent off the A52
The village is typical of many in this area of Nottinghamshire and, down the years, it has managed to maintain its rural character. Back in medieval times, Orston had one of the finest gypsum workings in the country though all that remains today of the Royal Plaster Works is a partially filled in pit in the centre of the village and some overgrown ponds on the outskirts.

Also just outside the village is the site of a mill and records show that there was a mill here as long ago as 1216. However, in 1916, the last mill on the site was dismantled and shipped, literally, half way round the world to New Zealand where is found a certain amount of fame as the country's first working windmill.

Scarrington   Map 4 ref D6
8 miles S of Newark-on-Trent off the A52
The main attraction of this small village is not a grand house or a splendid village church but a remarkable man-made edifice. A pile of around 50,000 horseshoes towers 17 feet high and was built by the former blacksmith, Mr Flinders. Over the years, souvenir hunters have taken the odd shoe here and there, with the result that the monument is bending over very slightly at the top.

However, the obelisk which Mr Flinders began in 1945, stands rock solid though all he used to bond the shoes was his skill and a great deal of luck! At one time it was coveted by an American visitor who wished to buy it and transport it to the United States.

Car Colston   Map 4 ref D6
8 miles SW of Newark-on-Trent off the A46
Now a conservation area, this village is fortunate in that it has remained unspoilt by modern development. Of particular interest

here are the village's two greens which both date from the reign of Elizabeth I. At that time individual strips of land were cultivated by the villagers and the typical ridge and furrow appearance can still be made out. In 1598, the parish was enclosed, the land being turned into the fenced fields that are now common today, but the land in the middle of the village was left open so that the villagers could graze their cattle. The Large Green, at 16 1/2 acres, is the largest in the county and, at the other end of the village lies Little Green (a mere 5 1/2 acres).

There are several interesting houses in the village but Old Hall Farm, which dates from 1812, is probably the one which receives most attention. The interest is directed, not at the building itself, but a former inhabitant, Robert Thoroton, who, in 1677, published *Antiquities of Nottinghamshire*. The first major history of the county, the work was updated in the late 18th century by John Throsby and it remains today one of the prime sources of local historians.

Screveton   *Map 4 ref D6*
7 miles SW of Newark-on-Trent off the A46

The ancient village, whose name means farm belonging to the sheriff, has a delightful, small 13th-century church which lies in a secluded position some way from the village. Reached by a footpath, the **Church of St Wilfrid** is home to a fine alabaster tomb of Richard Whalley with his three wives and 25 children at his feet.

The Whalleys were the principal family in the village for generations and it was probably at Screveton that Edward Whalley was born, though no one knows his date of birth. A wealthy woollen draper, as soon as the Civil War broke out, Edward joined the Parliamentarian cause - not a surprising decision as he was a cousin of Oliver Cromwell and also related to the Hacker family by marriage. However, Edward was the only Roundhead in a staunchly Royalist family.

Edward rose through the ranks of the Parliamentarian army and, in 1647, he was deployed to Hampton Court to guard the imprisoned Charles I. However, Edward allowed the king to escape, though in his defence Edward said it was to foil an assassination attempt. The king was recaptured and Edward stood as one of his judges at trail and signed the death warrant.

Successfully serving in Cromwell's government, following the Restoration Edward fled to Switzerland and found refuge among the puritan descendants of the Pilgrim Fathers. Little is known of his life after leaving England though many stories have been told and it is thought that he died in either 1674 or 1675.

Hawksworth
Map 4 ref D6

6 miles S of Newark-on-Trent off the A46

One of a number of attractive villages in the Vale of Belvoir, Hawksworth is well worth a detour. The 16th-century stone manor house still has its mid-17th-century dovecote and the church is much older that it first appears. The base of the tower was constructed in the 13th century of stone but the upper stories were added during the 17th century. However, inside is part of an intricately carved Saxon cross and, in the tower's south wall is a Norman tympanum.

Running along the northern village boundary is an ancient trackway, Long Hedge Lane, which runs from Bottesford to the ferry at Hazelford on the River Trent.

Sibthorpe
Map 4 ref D6

5 miles S of Newark-on-Trent off the A46

All that remains above ground of a priests' college, founded here in the 14th century, is the parish church and a **Dovecote**. Found in the middle of a field and some 60 feet high, this circular stone building has a tiled roof and nesting places for over 1,200 birds.

Of the three archbishops which Nottinghamshire has sent to Canterbury, Thomas Cranmer is, by far, the most well known but Sibthorpe was the childhood home of Thomas Secker (Archbishop 1758-68). Though Secker did not publish any works he was considered a scholar of his times and he was also a doctor of medicine.

Flintham
Map 4 ref D6

5 miles SW of Newark-on-Trent off the A46

Little has changed in this quiet village over the years though the style of late 20th century living has meant that most of the village shops are now shut. Once all the cottages in the village were owned by the occupants of Flintham Hall, but Flintham's life as an estate village has also gone. A great Victorian manor house, **Flintham Hall** has a conservatory that resembles Crystal Palace and it is considered one of the finest in the country. Still very much a family home, parts of the building date back to the 17th century, while some of the brickwork dates even further back to the Middle Ages.

Elston
Map 4 ref D6

3 miles SW of Newark-on-Trent off the A46

Surrounded by agricultural land, farming in Elston still continues but many of this compact and friendly village's occupants commute to work. As a consequence, the local trade of skep-making, or basket-making, using especially grown willows, has all but died out.

Evidence of early dwellers in the area has been found in the form of Stone Age flint and Roman pottery - not surprising as the village lies close to Fosse Way. However, little of Elston's early history has been documented though there has been one famous family living here. **Elston Hall** was owned by the Darwin family from 1680 to as recently as 1952 and this was where Erasmus Darwin was born in 1731. He went on to become one of England's finest physicians as well as an inventor and founder member of the Lunar Society. Most, though, will be more familiar with the works of Erasmus's grandson, Charles, who put forward the theory of evolution. Rather uncharitably, Charles has been recorded as claiming that his theory owned nothing to the work of his pioneering grandfather.

Another interesting building in the village is **Elston Chapel**; a building whose origins have been shrouded in mystery until recent research put forward the suggestion that the building was the chapel to the hospital of St Leonard that existed in this locality and was sold in 1576.

East Stoke   *Map 4 ref D6*
4 miles SW of Newark-on-Trent on the A46
The village is the site of the last great conflict of the War of the Roses: the Battle of Stoke Fields took place here on 16th June 1487. The battle saw the army of Henry VII defeated the Yorkists in a bloody battle that lasted for three hours and resulted in 7,000 deaths. The defeated army fled to the river across the meadow known today as the Red Gutter. Many of those who died on battle lie in Deadman's Field nearby, and local farmers have occasionally uncovered swords and other relics from the battle when ploughing their fields. Although the Wars of the Roses was, strictly speaking, between the rival houses of York and Lancaster, the intermittent warfare was exacerbated by the gentry and other aristocratic feuds. In this respect, the Wars of the Roses, which took place during the reign of a rather weak monarch, Henry VI, were a series of civil wars.

Though the battle site is the main attraction in the village, East Stoke has a history which goes back to the days of the Roman occupation. The Fosse Way, which divides the village into two, was originally part of the great Roman road from Bath to Lincoln and East Stoke is thought to be the site of the Roman fort of Ad Pontem. Mentioned in the Domesday Book, the manor of Stoke received the addition of East to distinguish it from Stoke Bardolph and not, as some local tales have suggested, to differentiate it from the old village which was deserted following the plague.

North and East of Newark-on-Trent

Coddington   *Map 4 ref E5*
2 miles E of Newark-on-Trent off the A17

This was the village from which Prince Rupert led his attack on Newark to relieve the town from the siege of 1644. A wander around the village today will still reveal some of the Civil War earthworks which were built to provide protection to the troops.

Brough   *Map 4 ref E5*
4 miles NE of Newark-on-Trent on the A46

The village, which lies on the Fosse Way, was the site of ***Crocolana***, one of the four Roman forts in Nottinghamshire which lay along the major route.

CHAPTER THREE
Industrial Nottinghamshire

Bentinck Monument, Mansfield

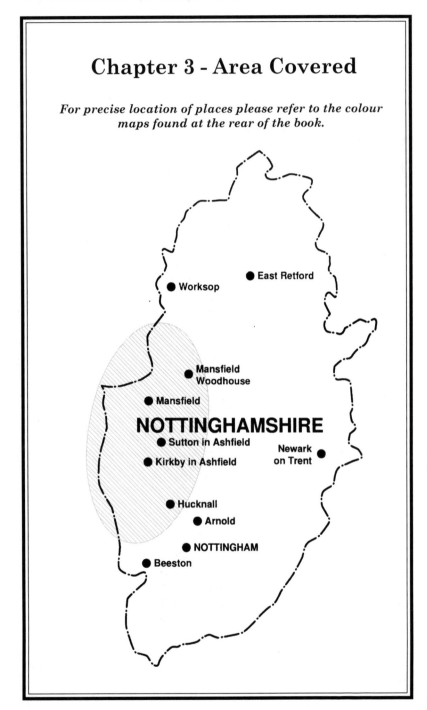

Chapter 3 - Area Covered

For precise location of places please refer to the colour maps found at the rear of the book.

● East Retford

● Worksop

● Mansfield Woodhouse

● Mansfield

NOTTINGHAMSHIRE

● Sutton in Ashfield

Newark on Trent ●

● Kirkby in Ashfield

● Hucknall

● Arnold

● NOTTINGHAM

● Beeston

3
Industrial Nottinghamshire

Introduction

This area of Nottinghamshire, which lies close to the border with Derbyshire, was dominated by the coal mining industry, but sadly, this is now greatly reduced today. Once part of the great Forest of Sherwood, coal has been mined here for centuries though, until the late 18th century, this was always on a small scale. As Nottingham and the surrounding towns and villages became an important centre for the textile industry, chiefly hosiery but later there were some cotton mills, the need for reliable energy sources grew.

Rural market towns expanded into industrial towns and their whole character changed as quick and cheap terraced housing was built for the influx of workers coming to jobs in the mills and the mines. The landscape also changed; though the forest and other land was cleared to make way for buildings and mines. During this time many agricultural communities were lost forever as the labourers moved to the more lucrative factories. Transportation was also important and the Erewash Canal was started in 1777 to take coal from the fields to the River Trent. Once a hive of activity the canal fell into disrepair in the 1920s but it is now, once again, bustling though this time with pleasure craft.

Into this grim life was born DH Lawrence in 1885; his father was a miner at the Brinsley pit and the family lived in a terraced house in Eastwood. Drawing on his childhood experiences, Lawrence's novels give a true insight into the lives of those living in a colliery town at the beginning of the 20th century. By contrast, the landowners made their fortunes and there are several fine houses in the area including the home of the poet Lord Byron, Newstead Abbey.

Eastwood

This town is very much an industrial town, dominated by the coal mining industry. A close knit community, the town is best known as the birthplace, in 1885, of David Herbert Lawrence. The Lawrence family home, a two up, two down, terrace house in Victoria Street is now the *DH Lawrence Birthplace Museum* and it has been furnished in a late 19th-century style with which the Lawrence family would have been familiar. There are also some household items on display which belonged to the family and anyone visiting the museum will see that the house's front window is larger than others in the same street. This is where Mrs Lawrence displayed the children's cloths and other linen items which she made and sold to supplement the fluctuating wages brought home by her miner husband.

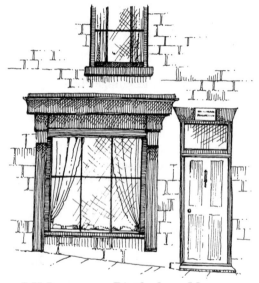

DH Lawrence Birthplace Museum

In 1887, the Lawrence family moved to a larger, end of terrace house in Eastwood which today is known as the *Sons and Lovers Cottage* as it featured as the Morels' house, The Bottoms, in Lawrence's novel. This house too is open to the public, though by appointment only, and is also laid out with furnishings and artefacts which are appropriate to the times. Lawrence's father was a miner at the nearby Brinsley Pit and though the family moved house in Eastwood several times, the Lawrences remained short of money. First attending the local school, Lawrence was the first Eastwood boy to gain a scholarship to Nottingham High School, where he was a pupil until 1901. Lawrence started his working life as a clerk before undertaking a teacher training course and moving to Croydon to begin life as a teacher.

Though Lawrence had already begun writing, his major novels were not written until after 1912, the year he eloped with his former professor's wife and left England. Leaning heavily on the influences of his upbringing in Eastwood, *Sons and Lovers*, first published in 1913, not only describes the countryside around Eastwood but also portrays many local personalities and such were the descriptions of, amongst others, Lawrence senior that there was a great deal of local resentment when the novel came out in print.

Lawrence and his wife, Frieda Weekley, returned to England during World War I but they were unable to settle and were soon travelling abroad again. In the early 1920s, Lawrence published *Women in Love* and, a few years later, was diagnosed with tuberculosis, the disease from which he died in 1930. It was whilst in Florence, trying unsuccessfully to find a cure for his crippling condition, that Lawrence wrote his most famous novel, *Lady Chatterley's Lover*. First published in 1928, the full text of the controversial story was not printed until 1960 and, even then, it was the subject of a court case which is almost as famous as the book.

The **Erewash Canal**, completed in 1779, runs close to Eastwood and it provided an efficient form of transport for the coal away from the numerous pits in this area. At Shipley Lock, in the town, an aqueduct carries the canal over the River Erewash and it was constructed by first building the aqueduct and then diverting the river to run underneath. In the 1980s, following years of neglect, the canal was cleared and made suitable for use by pleasure craft whilst the towpath was resurfaced and it is now a pleasant and interesting walk.

Just to the east of Eastwood lies **Greasley**, once a village in its own right but now almost entirely engulfed by its neighbour. Dating back to the days of the Normans, when it was known as Griseleia and possessed both a church and a priest, the village did not follow the normal layout of the time with a village green and duckpond though there are some very pleasant cottages still to be seen. Little is known of Greasley until the 14th century when Nicholas de Cantelupe fortified his manor house adjoining the church. The house became known as **Greasley Castle** and, today, the traces of the moat and walls can still be seen at Castle Farm.

It was also Nicholas de Cantelupe who, in 1345, founded **Greasley Priory** for the Carthusian order. The house fell into disrepair after the Dissolution and many of the village buildings have some of the priory's stone in their construction. Each year, in May, a procession of local clergymen, followed by their congregation, walk from the local Roman Catholic church to the priory ruins to hold a service. Standing on a site which has held a church for over 1,000 years, St Mary's Church has, in its parish records of 1603, the marriage of John Robinson. He was a pastor to the Pilgrim Fathers and Robinson also gave a farewell address before the Fathers set sail on the *Mayflower*.

Well known as the birthplace of DH Lawrence, Eastwood also has its place in local history as the birthplace of the Midlands County Railway. It was on 16th August 1832 at **The Sun Inn** where a meeting of wealthy coal merchants decided the future transport of coal from local mines to the chief markets of the day lay in rail transport. Hence the Leicester to Swannington line was built and the Midlands County Railway was born.

The Sun Inn

The Sun Inn was built in 1750 and today provides excellent facilities for visitors and offers comprehensive conference amenities in a location convenient for the M1 and within easy access to the beautiful scenery of the Derbyshire Peak District. The Sun Inn has 15 superbly presented en-suite bedrooms with all amenities and caters for family requirements. This is one of the Hardys and Hansons houses which offers a good value menu with additional blackboard specials and dishes for vegetarians and children. The wine list features a popular range wines at sensible prices. *The Sun Inn Hotel, 6 Derby Road, Eastwood, Nottinghamshire NG16 3NT Tel: 01773 712940*

South and East of Eastwood

Kimberley
Map 3 ref B6

1 mile S of Eastwood on the A610

The town lies on the **Robin Hood Way**, a 88 mile long footpath devised by the Nottingham Wayfarers' Rambling Club to celebrated its golden jubilee in 1988. Beginning at Nottingham Castle, the path takes in many of the places associated with the legendary hero before reaching its end at St Mary's Church, Edwinstowe, where Robin Hood is said to have married Maid Marian.

The Stag Inn

The half-timbered **Stag Inn** is situated on the edge of Kimberley town centre on the main Nottingham road. Dating back to the early 18th century, this impressive family orientated pub was originally a farmhouse; it then became a coaching inn with a blacksmith's attached which was known as The Reindeer until the 1860s. Since taking over in 1994, landlords Karen and Neil Murden have created a superb establishment where a warm welcome is assured. The refurbished interior has a wonderful atmosphere, with quarry-tiled floors, beamed ceilings, pew-style seating, and an unusual collection of early fruit machines. Children are most welcome and to the rear is an attractive, safe playarea. *The Stag Inn, 67 Nottingham Road, Kimberley, Nottinghamshire NG16 2NB Tel: 0115 938 3151*

Awsworth
Map 3 ref B6

1 miles S of Eastwood on the A6096

In order to lay the tracks for the Great Northern Railway line from Derby to Nottingham, a viaduct was need to carry the railway over the Erewash Canal, the River Erewash, and the Nottingham Canal which all lie close to Awsworth. The resulting construction, built in 1876-7, is still an impressive sight though the line is now disused. One of only two viaducts in England to be made of wrought iron lattice girders, the **Bennerley Viaduct** has 16 spans which are set on pillars 56 feet high.

Cossall
Map 3 ref B6

3 miles S of Eastwood off the A6096

Now a conservation area, this village has some notable buildings such as the Willoughby almshouses and a farmhouse which includes part of the original home of the Willoughby family. They were a branch of the Willoughbys of Wollaton, a dynasty that was founded by a wealthy 13th-century wool merchant from Nottingham named Ralph Bugge. This rather unfortunate name (which means hob-goblin) was, understandably, changed by his descendants to the more acceptable Willoughby; a name taken from the village of Willoughby-on-the-Wolds on the border with Leicestershire, where Ralph owned a fair share of land.

Cossall was another of DH Lawrence's haunts and it also featured in his novel *The Rainbow* as the village of Cossethay, home of the Brangwen family. The fictional character, William Brangwen, is said to have been based on Alfred Burrows, whose daughter Lawrence courted for some time. The Burrows family lived in a cottage near to the charming village church.

Trowell
Map 3 ref B7

3 miles S of Eastwood off the A6096

To many people travelling up and down the M1 motorway, Trowell is just a service station, somewhere to stop and take a break, but the village, which lies close to the county border with Derbyshire, dates back to well before the days of the motorcar. First mentioned in the Domesday Book as Torwell, a name which means the well on the hill, the village was quite a settlement, with at least 15 wells and, according to the Norman survey, a priest and half a church. Several of the county's most well known families have been associated with Trowell including the De Trowells, the Willoughby family, and their descendants, the Middletons.

Little changed in this quiet area until the coming of the railways and, in 1884, a new station was opened in the village allowing its inhabitants the opportunity to travel more widely. The moors around Trowell had been mined for coal from the 13th century and it was not until 1926 that the Trowell colliery ceased production. The other key industry of the immediate area was iron. The abundance of coal and the nearby River Erewash provided the other materials needed in a forge and, in the late 19th century, the village saw an influx of ironworkers from the Black Country coming to work in the forges. However, village life was not been completely swept away by the industrial age. The oldest building in Trowell is undoubtedly its beautiful old **St Helen's Church**. Dating from the 13th century, the remains of a previous Anglo-Saxon building were found in the chancel during some renovation work.

Finally, in 1951, Trowell was chosen as the Festival Village for the Festival of Britain as not only was it situated in the centre of England but it also blended together rural and industrial life.

Since last appearing in *Hidden Places*, **The Festival Inn** has been purchased by the Tom Cobleigh chain of inns and, in 1995, it was completely refurbished. On entering, visitors will be aware of the warmth and hospitality displayed by the staff and the general ambience of the inn. First impressions are so vital and once seated visitors can take in the decor and furnishings, from the fine carved wooden wall-to-ceiling alcoves to the feature fireplace and the stained glass lighting surrounds.

The Festival Inn

No one coming to The Festival Inn will be able to escape the wonderful aroma of home-cooked food and there is a comprehensive menu as well as a list of daily specials and an excellent carvery from which guests can make their choice. The Festival caters for all age groups and families and there are lots of other things happening here including Friday Night Live, featuring all kinds of live music. The function and banqueting facilities are first class and are catered for in either the Phoenix Suite or Harry's Bar. Phone for details of entertainment and special deals. *The Festival Inn, Ilkeston Road, Trowell, Nottinghamshire NG9 3PX Tel: 0115 932 2691*

Bestwood
Map 3 ref C6

6 miles E of Eastwood off the B683

Once part of the Royal hunting park of Bestwood, it was whilst staying at **Bestwood Lodge** that Richard III heard of Henry Tudor's invasion of Wales in 1485. The king left his lodge and was killed defending his crown at the Battle of Bosworth Field. The village's royal connections did not, however, die with King Richard. Bestwood was also a favourite hunting ground of Charles II and he enjoyed staying here with Nell Gwynne. One local story tells of a wager the king struck with Nell, saying she could have all the land she could ride around before breakfast. Nell, not known for being an early riser, made an exception and, the next morning, she rose at dawn and rode through the countryside surrounding the village dropping handkerchiefs along the way. Arriving back before breakfast, Nell is said to have won the wager and Charles kept his side of the bargain. Whether or not the story is true, Nell certain was given substantial quantities of land in the area and her son, by the king, became the 1st Duke of St Albans. The present Bestwood Lodge was built by the 10th Duke of St Albans on a low hill. Begun in 1862, the lodge is a grand house with flying buttresses, gables, and chimneys, and it best feature is undoubtedly the loft entrance tower with its high pyramidal roof.

By the 18th century, the lands of the royal hunting grounds were being broken up into farms and only a small area was left forested. Two mills were built taking power from the River Leen and, in 1872, the 10th Duke of St Albans leased some land to John Lancaster who sank a mine shaft. The village expanded to accommodate the new workers and their families arriving to work in the mills and the mine. The first colliery houses were built in 1876 and soon the Bestwood Coal and Iron Village was established with all those living there dependent on the company. Although the colliery closed down in 1967 the spoil heap can still be seen though now it is grassed over and is a true haven for wildlife. Now called the **Bestwood Country Park**, the land also includes areas of the old royal hunting park and the 450 acres offer many differing landscapes.

One of the best views of the **Bestwood Winding House** can be found in the country park. A listed building, the winding house, along with the headstocks, still stand even following the closure of the colliery. Unique in that it has a steam driven vertical winding engine, the house lies to the north of the colliery's old spoil heap.

Also at Bestwood can be found the **Model Aviation Centre**, a museum which specialises in accurate models of aircraft of up to half the scale of the original machine. As well as seeing the finished models, visitors can watch them fly and also see models in various stages of construction.

North of Eastwood

Brinsley

Map 3 ref A6

2 miles N of Eastwood on the A608

In 1872 the colliery here needed a second shaft and this was sunk to a depth of 780 feet. To enable the miners to be raised and lowered up and down the pit two headstocks were also erected. Though the colliery ceased production in the 1930s, the shafts were kept open until 1970 to allow access to neighbouring pits. Finally, the pit closed, the buildings were all demolished, and the site landscaped for a picnic area. The **Headstocks**, however, were re-erected on the site and they are the centrepiece of a number of Lawrence trails. Winner of Best Pub Food category in the Nottinghamshire County

The Yew Tree

Council Leisure Services Tourism Awards, **The Yew Tree** is a perfect calling point for food and refreshment. The pub can be found situated on the A608 though the village 1 mile from junction 27 on the M1. Hosts Tony and Denise have been winning awards for quite a number of years now, so it comes as no surprise to find really enjoyable home-cooked food prepared by chef Tony, with a huge choice on the menu that includes over 20 fresh fish dishes. On alternate Saturdays the pub hosts speciality nights for many occasions and 1960s and 1970s discos every Wednesday. Children are welcome and there is reasonable access for wheelchairs. Opening and catering hours vary a little so for those travelling a distance it is best to telephone first but the journey is well worth it. *The Yew Tree, Cordy Lane, Brinsley, Nottinghamshire NG16 5BY Tel: 01773 715881*

Underwood   Map 3 ref A6
2 miles N of Eastwood on the B600

Coal has been mined in the village and surrounding area from the time of the Middle Ages though other industries, including ironstone mining, framework knitting, and brick manufacturing, have also provided some employment. In the late 19th century, the shaft of an earlier pit was deepened and the rows of terraced houses were built. The pit is now closed but Underwood still retains many of the characteristics of a mining community and the pit headstocks now stand in the churchyard.

In the village can also be seen the Elizabethan chimneys of Felley Priory, which is now a private house. Founded in 1165, local legend has it that a tunnel ran from this Augustinian foundation to nearby Wansley Hall (now in ruins). Whether this is true or not, the two places are known to have close associations dating from the Middle Ages.

Jessie Chambers, a friend of DH Lawrence and the person believed to have been the inspiration for Miriam in *Sons and Lovers*, taught at Underwood School and Lawrence certainly knew the countryside around the village.

Somercotes Selston   Map 3 ref A5
4 miles N of Eastwood on the B600

Mentioned in the Domesday Book as a place with a church and three acres of meadows, like many other village communities in this western area of Nottinghamshire, Somercotes Selston was very much a farming community. Also like many places along the Derbyshire border, under the fertile agricultural land lay coal and, as early as 1206, leases for coal mining were granted. For centuries the coal mining operation remained small scale but, by the 1850s, Somercotes Selston had taken on many of the aspects of a modern colliery village. Other industries which many families found useful in supplementing the family income were ironstone mining and framework knitting. The last coal pit in Somercotes Selston closed in 1956 and, since then, the village has, very much, taken on the air of a commuter village.

Beside the beautiful Norman **Church of St Helen**, which commands splendid views out over the neighbouring Derbyshire hills, is a neatly tendered graveyard which is also the last resting place of Dan Boswell, the king of the gypsies. For many years new born gypsy babies were always brought to Boswell's gravestone to be baptised and many would come to the church to pay their respects.

Annesley Woodhouse
Map 3 ref B5

5 miles NE of Eastwood on the A608

All that remains of the old village of Annesley is Annesley Hall, the home of Mary Chaworth a lady for whom Lord Byron formed an early affection, and the roofless ruins of the old village church. By contrast the church, in the newer part of village known as Annesley Woodhouse, is modern and it replaces an earlier church which is believed to have been burnt down by Suffragettes. From this church there are views over the woods, fields, the local golf course, and Annesley Colliery where two long rows of houses, known as The Rows can still be seen.

Newstead
Map 3 ref B5

5 miles NE of Eastwood off the A608

The village of Newstead, often overlooked for the famous abbey which lies close by, is another example of a colliery village. The terrace houses were built for the miners and their families working at the nearby pits belonging to the Byron family.

The grand mansion house, **Newstead Abbey**, lies just to the east of the village and this was, famously, the home of the poet, Lord Byron and his ancestors for many years. Originally, Newstead was a true place of worship when, in the late 12th century an Augustinian priory was founded here by Henry II in atonement for his part in the death of Thomas à Becket. However, most of the medieval remains that can still be seen date from building work which was carried out some 100 years after the abbey's foundation. The abbey was bought, in 1539, by Sir John Byron, who converted the monastic buildings for his own private use. Despite destroying much of the building somewhat surprisingly a statue of Christ still stands above the main entrance hall and there is also a statue of the Virgin and Child in the gable.

Though the Byron family have lived here since the mid-16th century and added a whole new wing, the family was beset by money troubles due, in some part, to their own extravagances. One of the more colourful characters within the family, the 5th Lord Byron, known as Devil Byron, not only enjoyed playing with a warship on the lake but was involved in the killing of one of his neighbours during a drunken brawl in a London tavern: though the lord was acquitted of murder. By the time the 5th Lord Byron died the scullery was the only room in this huge mansion that did not have a leaking roof and this was were his body was found. The poet Lord Byron, the 5th lord's great nephew, then succeeded to the title and began, with some success, to make some of the rooms habitable but he too ran out of money and was forced, in 1817, to sell the house.

The magnificent Newstead Abbey owes as much to the priors and the Byrons as it does to its subsequent owner Colonel Wildman who carried out some much needed renovation work. In 1931, the house was given to the City of Nottingham. Though the abbey welcomes many visitors throughout the year the grounds still contain a wealth of hidden places. There is a secret garden, a beautifully carved fountain decorated with fantastic animals, the elaborate memorial to Byron's dog Boatswain, and the large lake where the 5th lord re-enacted naval battles. The house, home to the **Byron Museum**, too is well worth a visit and a tour around the many rooms reveals a whole host of splendid treasures.

Although Newstead Abbey has had many interesting occupants it is still best known as the home of the poet and many of his relics can be seen inside. Born in 1788 and baptised George Gordon, the poet's mother, Catherine Gordon, was abandoned by her husband Captain Mad Jack Byron before George's birth and the child was brought up in Aberdeen in relative poverty as his father had spent Catherine's fortune before his premature death in 1791. Following the death of the 5th lord, George succeeded to the title at the age of 10 and such was the state of Newstead Abbey that he lived elsewhere in the county. Educated at Harrow and Cambridge, Byron did not forget the poverty he had seen at first hand during his childhood and, for his maiden speech in the House of Lords, he took up the framework knitters' cause.

Following the completion of his education, Byron travelled widely in Europe and the Middle East where he found inspiration for many of his works. After a long courtship, he married Annabella Milbanke in 1815 but they separated within a year of the marriage and, from this time onwards, Byron became notorious for his excesses. Such were the nature of his love affairs that, once the darling of London society, Byron found himself ostracised and he went into a self-imposed exile and never returned to England again. Before the completion of his work, *Don Juan*, Byron was struck down with a fever in Greece from which he died in 1824. His body was brought back to England and, after being refused a burial at Westminster Abbey, he was finally laid to rest in the graveyard of Hucknall church.

Built in 1881 at the time of the rapidly developing railways, **The Station Hotel** played host to many visitors in this once bustling mining community until the closure of the line with the Beeching Axe! Although the hotel survived, the mining industry was dramatically reduced. But four years ago, a new adventure with the railways began with the reopening of the Mansfield to Nottingham line. Avril and Marvyn have been at The Station Hotel as tenants and managers for the past seven years. This substantial building with its black and white timbered front, still caters for locals and

The Station Hotel

visitors alike and has a very homely atmosphere. The Station prides itself on a great selection of ales, all kept in excellent condition and with a good choice of lagers. Children are welcome and there's a good outdoor play area. Railway enthusiasts will enjoy the memorabilia. *The Station Hotel, Station Road, Newstead Village, Nottinghamshire NG15 0BZ Tel: 01623 753294*

Linby   *Map 3 ref B6*
5 miles NE of Eastwood on the A6011

Situated on the banks of the River Leen, during the late 18th century the riverbank was a busy, bustling place with six cotton mills being powered by the water. The mills were strictly functional but George Robinson, their owner, did not want to be out done by his near neighbours at Newstead Abbey and he added battlements and other ornate features and, thus, gave Castle Mill its name. Young apprentices were brought in from as far away as London to work in Castle Mill. Housed in small lodges near to the mill, the children worked long hours weaving cotton cloth in terrible conditions with minimal food and clothing provided. Brought to work in the mills from a young age (some were no more than 10 years old) many found the life too hard and they can be found buried in the local churchyard.

When the 5th Lord Byron dammed the River Leen upstream from Linby, in order to create a lake on his estate, he also played havoc with the water supply to the mills. With a reduction in power, the Robinsons had to find another reliable power source and, in 1786, they were the first to apply steam power to a cotton mill when they installed a Boulton and Watt engine.

Papplewick
Map 3 ref B6
6 miles NE of Eastwood on the B683

This pretty village, half of which is designated a conservation area, still retains many pink stone cottages and the trappings of the industrial age have been, almost totally, lost. Back in the 18th century, life was much different in this now quiet village: the cotton mills at Papplewick and nearby Linby being witness to some of the worst excesses of child labour.

Lying at the southern boundary of Sherwood Forest and just south of Newstead Abbey, the village is the starting point for several footpaths leading on to these famous lands. Along one such footpath, walkers, with the permission of the owner, can have a look at a cave known as **Robin Hood's Stable**. It was here that the folk hero stabled his horses ready for forays into Nottingham.

Although the grand splendour of Newstead Abbey lies not far way, the village has a most outstanding building of its own, **Papplewick Hall**. First occupied in 1787 and built by the Adams brothers, the village cricket pitch can be found adjacent to the hall. The village **Church of St James** also has some interesting features including, inside the 14th-century tower, a musicians' gallery. The squire's pew has its own fireplace and it is said that one particular squire, when he thought the sermon had gone on long enough, would bang on the fire irons as a signal to the vicar to finish his address.

To the east of the village can be found **Papplewick Pumping Station**, a great Victorian landmark that is fast becoming one of the better known attractions in an area dominated by legendary characters and coal mines. Built in the late 19th century, its original purpose was to supply water to the expanding city and suburbs of Nottingham but it is now part of a system that has long been overtaken by 20th century technology. Lovingly restored by a dedicated group of enthusiasts, the pumping station is open to the public on Sunday afternoons during the summer. Housing two beam engines by James Watt and Company and powered by six Lancaster boilers, in its heyday the station could pump 3 million gallons of water a day! Apart from the fascinating machinery, the splendid Victorian cast iron columns and galleries as well as the stained glass make this one of the more interesting industrial sites to visit. Outside, in front of the red brick engine room is a large cooling pool and the surrounding grounds have been landscaped.

Hucknall   *Map 3 ref B6*
4 miles NE of Eastwood off the A611

Following his death, in 1824, in Greece, Lord Byron was brought back to England and buried in the family vault at Hucknall church.

The Station Hotel

The Station Hotel, situated in the town, epitomises the scale and style of hotels which sprang up to service the needs of passengers on the new railways in the 1800s. The hotel has five good sized letting rooms which are available all year round and the hotel offers a good base for those touring the area or for businessmen looking for a good stop-over point. David and Shirley are the friendly hosts and they welcome families and offer assistance to any disabled guests. Food is served during normal opening hours and a specials board lists the dishes of the day. There is also a special three course lunch available on Sundays. AA Listed. *The Station Hotel, Station Terrace, Hucknall, Nottinghamshire NG15 7TQ Tel: 0115 963 2588*

Mansfield

Lying close to the Robin Hood country and near to Lord Byron's splendid ancestral home, this old market town has plenty to offer the visitor. In the heart of the town, a plaque and new tree mark the historic centre of Sherwood Forest and the famous place where Robin Hood first encountered Friar Tuck lies just outside the town at Rainworth Water. Of the stories and songs that have been told over the years about the mysterious forest one ballad tells the story of a miller and a king. Whilst out hunting in Sherwood Forest Henry II found himself lost and fortunately found a miller, John Cockle, who failed to recognise him. Being a hospitable man, Cockle offered the king some venison pie but asked him not to let on that they made free with the royal deer. So amused was Henry II with the miller's simple country ways that he made Cockle a forest overseer, gave him £300 a year, and made him a knight. Further along Westgate is **Cromwell House**, named after Dr Samuel Cromwell who lived here for some 40 years in the late 17th and early 18th centuries and the house may have been built for him as it dates from around the 1680s.

The old market place, which still holds markets on Mondays, Thursdays, Fridays, and Saturdays, is also the centre of Mansfield and around the square can be seen some of the town's more interesting buildings. Pride of place, however, goes to the impressive Gothic **Bentinck Monument** erected in 1848 in memory of Lord George Bentinck. The younger son of the Duke of Portland, Bentinck was a long serving Member of Parliament and a great friend of Disraeli. Funds for the memorial were raised by public subscription but they unfortunately ran out before the finishing touch, a statue of Bentinck himself, could be placed in the central space. The original market cross, dating from the 16th or 17th century, lies in Westgate. As well as the Moot Hall, built in 1752 by Lady Oxford, Waverley House, which lies close by and dates from the same period, is an interesting mixture of architectural styles.

During the 17th century, Mansfield was noted for its nonconformist leanings and, in Stockwell Gate, is the **Old Meeting House** and parsonage, which date from the early 18th century. Much altered over the years and with some splendid William Morris stained glass added, this is one of the oldest chapels still in use in the county. There has been a place of worship on the site of the present parish **Church of St Peter and St Paul** since the time of the Domesday Book. The church standing today was built over many years and some of its stones are thought to have come from a Saxon building.

Found just to the northwest of the market place, **Mansfield Museum** concentrates its collections largely on local interest, including a model of a Roman villa that once stood at nearby Mansfield Woodhouse. The collection spans the centuries from that early occupation right up to more recent times, with pictures and artefacts relating to the industry of the town and surrounding villages. The adjoining art gallery also carries a local theme and features works by artists of the area including the watercolourist AS Buxton, who is well known for his works of Mansfield.

Further west, on the outskirts of the town centre lies the **Metal Box Factory** which grew out of a mustard business that was established in the 1830s by David Cooper Barringer. In order to keep the mustard dry, the company began to store the powder in metal boxes and not the traditional wooden crates and, by the late 19th century, the market for decorated metal box packaging had grown so great that the company decided to concentrate on the production of the boxes rather than the milling of mustard.

One feature though, which anyone approaching Mansfield cannot fail to miss, is the enormous railway viaduct which dominates the skyline. Built in 1875, the 15 immense stone arches cut through the heart of the town and it is one of the largest viaducts in an English town.

The Imperial Bar

The Imperial Bar is a great place for the younger readers or the young at heart. For those looking for somewhere to enjoy themselves in pleasant surroundings, The Imperial is certainly a great place to visit, with lots of cd music, a resident disc jockey, and male and female dancers at weekends. Personally run by Trevor and Chantelle for the past four years, this is the place to be seen in, in Mansfield. The decor is stylish and the selection of beers, wines, and spirits extensive. There is no entrance fee and The Imperial Bar is open seven days a week. *The Imperial Bar, 28 Leeming Street, Mansfield, Nottinghamshire NG18 1NE Tel: 01623 646035*

Situated just three minutes drive from the town centre, **The Red Gate**, one of Hardys and Hansons excellent public houses, has experienced licensees at the helm. A warm welcome awaits all visitors from Peter and Jennifer who have been at the Red Gate for over 10 years and have 25 years experience in the trade, which is evident in the operation and presentation of the pub. Built on the

The Red Gate

site of an old bus garage 35 years ago, this is a place where visitors and locals can mix freely in convivial surroundings and enjoy a chat whilst sampling excellent Kimberley ales; bitter and mild are available and they have a brewery guest ale which changes six times a year. A few snacks are available at lunchtime. *The Red Gate, Westfield Lane, Mansfield, Nottinghamshire NG19 6EH Tel: 01623 24406*

Conveniently situated to the southwest of Mansfield on the A617, the impressive **Fringe Hotel** offers a lot more than just accommodation. This purpose built three crown hotel also boasts one of the finest leisure complexes outside London. Its many facilities include a fully equipped gymnasium, dance studio, solarium, saunas, and six squash courts, plus an old style snooker room and reading room. All these facilities, along with qualified instruction, are available to residents at no extra cost.

The hotel itself has 15 well-appointed guest rooms, each with its own en-suite bathroom, colour television, direct dial telephone, trouser press, and tea and coffee making facilities. There is also an attractive restaurant offering an impressive á la carte menu and a

Fringe Hotel

relaxing lounge serving a good selection of drinks and bar meals. *Fringe Hotel and Leisure Complex, Briar Lane, Mansfield, Nottinghamshire NG18 3HS Tel: 01623 641337 Fax: 01623 27521*

Greenwood Craft and Coffee Shop lies in the heart of Sherwood Forest just off the main A60 Mansfield to Nottingham road. The craft and garden centre is part of Portland College which was

Greenwood Craft and Coffee Shop

founded in 1946 to retrain people with disabilities for new jobs and aims to maximise abilities as well as minimising the effects of disability. Greenwood is open seven days a week, except Christmas and New Year, and has something to offer the whole family. The Friar Tuck's Trail, a woodland path that is approximately 2 1/2 miles long, leads visitors through the forest and, with the help of a guide sheet, there is plenty of flora and fauna to discover along the way. At the far western end of the trail lie the collapsed remains of Friar Tuck's Well and nearby is a moated site which possibly dates back to the time of the Norman conquest.

After a stroll round the trail, the coffee shop, which incorporates a craft shop, is the ideal place to rest a while. With freshly brewed coffee, steaming pots of tea, and home-made cakes and sandwiches whatever visitors choose will be a real treat. Staffed entirely by volunteers, and with an adventure playground for the children, Greenwood Craft and Coffee Shop is well worth a visit. *Greenwood Craft and Coffee Shop, Portland College, Nottingham Road, Mansfield, Nottinghamshire NG18 4TJ Tel: 01623 792141*

South and West of Mansfield

Skegby   *Map 3 ref B5*
2 miles W of Mansfield off the A6075

The village is lucky in having a particularly fine example of a 14th-century cruck cottage though this was not discovered until restoration work was taking place on the building in the 1950s. The village's pinfold, the place where stray animals were held until their owner claimed them, has also been restored and can be found on the Mansfield road. In the 17th century, Skegby was the home of Elizabeth Hooton, a Quaker of distinction, and her house was a regular meeting place.

Teversal   *Map 1 ref B4*
3 miles W of Mansfield off the B6014

The village is the fictional home of Lady Chatterley and the nearby woodlands of the Hardwick estate (the hall lies in Derbyshire) were the meeting place for her and the gamekeeper. In fact, Teversal could still be described as an oasis of rural calm set amidst many colliery villages.

Dating back well before the Norman Conquest, the first church here was Anglo-Saxon, this was a manorial village belonging to the Molyneux and the Carnarvon families. The Carnarvon family pew in the present ancient church has some particularly beautiful carvings which give it an appearance of a four-poster bed whilst the Molyneux crypt is another unusual feature found inside.

Sutton in Ashfield   Map 3 ref B5
2 miles SW of Mansfield on the A38

This once small village has grown over the years as a result of local coal mining though a few of the original village's 17th and 18th century cottages can be seen near the Church of St Mary Magdalene. At the heart of the old village, the church contains some Norman work on the west wall and much of the rest of the building was constructed in the Middle Ages.

The Snipe at Sutton is a Hardys and Hansons house and is an excellent example of a well run brewery owned inn and restaurant. Built in the early 1990s, it is obvious that a lot of thought and planning went into the design and construction. The presentation is interesting with attractive decor and furnishing. Gleaming brasswork, sparkling polished tables, and a smile from the welcoming staff will certainly add to the pleasure of a visit. The Snipe has already a

The Snipe at Sutton

good reputation for its food and there is plenty of choice. In addition to the standard but comprehensive menu, there are daily specials which can range from a large steak, jumbo mixed grill, and Beef Wellington to lighter meals. Visitors can choose from a fine array of well-kept ales, fine lagers, and bottled beers or the good choice of popular wines. Children are very welcome in the restaurant and the facilities for the disabled are excellent with special ramps, good wide door areas, toilets, and parking. Open all day 11.00 until 23.00 Monday to Saturday and 12.00 to 22.30 on Sunday. *The Snipe at Sutton, Alfreton Road, Sutton-in-Ashfield, Nottinghamshire NG17 1JE Tel: 01623 443604*

North of Mansfield

Clipstone   Map 1 ref C4
3 miles NE of Mansfield on the B6030

There is thought to have been a royal hunting lodge in this area of Sherwood Forest from as early as 1164 but the remains seen today are known as ***King John's Palace*** as he spent so much time here. Added to and substantially rebuilt in the 15th century, the hunting lodge fell into disrepair and, as quickly as, 1525 is was all but abandoned.

The walls left standing are thought to part of the chapel built by Edward I in 1279 and it was here, in 1290, that Edward held a parliament as indeed did King John in 1212. Though there is a decaying oak just 2 miles away known as ***Parliament Oak***, the palace is the more likely venue for the parliaments held at Clipstone.

Mansfield Woodhouse
2 miles N of Mansfield on the A60

Map 1 ref B4

Before the opening of Sherwood Colliery in 1903, Mansfield Woodhouse was a small and quiet rural village of farms and labourers' cottages. However, the village also had a remarkable number of large, grand houses as the area was considered to be a fashionable place to live.

Opposite The Cross, in the heart of Mansfield Woodhouse stands one of these fine houses, the Georgian ***Burnaby House***. Still retaining many of its original, elegant features the house was obviously built for a prosperous family and, during the mid-19th century, it was occupied by the Duke of Portland's land agent. On the other side of the road stands a stump which is all that remains of the Market Cross which was erected here after a great fire in 1304. The village stocks also stood close by and they were once used to imprison George Fox, the Quaker Movement founder, after he had preached the gospel to the villagers.

At the bottom of the street lies the oldest building in Mansfield Woodhouse, ***St Edmund's Church***. Most of the original church was lost, along with the parish records, when fire swept through the village in the early 14th century. The present church was built on the same site though it has undergone some severe restoration in the 19th century. Lying not far from the church is a manor house known as ***Woodhouse Castle*** because of the battlements which were added to the building in the early 1800s. Dating from the 17th century, this was the house of the Digby family and, in particular, General Sir John Digby, Sheriff of Nottingham, who found fame for the part he played in the Civil War.

Another building of note is the essentially 18th-century ***Wolfhunt House*** found just off the High Street. The unusual name is derived from a local legend which suggests that the land on which the house is built once belonged to a man who was employed to frighten away the wolves in Sherwood Forest by blowing a hunting horn.

Warsop

Map 1 ref C4

4 miles N of Mansfield on the A60

Now a large village, the original rural settlement of **Church Warsop** expanded in the 19th century with the opening of several local collieries and the building of nearby colliery villages. During the General Strike of 1926, some of the miners carried on working and this has lead to the local nickname of Scab Alley.

However, mining has not been the only industry in the area and it was lime from Warsop that was quarried and used in the restoration of Southwell Minster following the Civil War. Today, the scars of the shallow quarrying are barely visible but the areas of humpy ground, noted for their birds and wild flowers, now go by the name of the Hills and Holes.

Cuckney

Map 1 ref B3

6 miles N of Mansfield on the A632

An estate village to the country seat of the Dukes of Portland, Welbeck Abbey, Cuckney is made up of farm workers cottages. Along with Clumber House, Thoresby Hall, and Rufford Abbey, **Welbeck Abbey** makes up the four large estates in this area of Nottingham-

St Winifred's Church, Holbeck

shire which has become known as **The Dukeries**. It was the 5th duke who began, in 1854, an extensive building programme that turned Welbeck into what is seen today. The most impressive of his additions was the riding school, the second largest in the world, complete with a peat floor and gas jet lighting. The building is now in the hands of the Ministry of Defence and it is used as an Army training college, though the abbey and the grounds have been maintained in perfect condition. The *Dukeries Adventure Park and Picnic Area*, on the Welbeck estate, provides all manner of supervised outdoor activities including rock climbing.

A keen racing man, the 6th duke both bred and reared racehorses at his own stud in the nearby estate village of *Holbeck*. Winning many races, including three classics, the duke's famous stallion, St Simon, is still remembered in the racing world today. As well as holding great house parties, the duke of a well-known host, he also built, in 1915, a beautiful new church in the village. *St Winifred's Church*, named after his wife, the duchess, is well worth a visit and, in the churchyard, are several family graves.

Back in Cuckney itself, there is a large mound in the churchyard which represents the site where, in the mid-12th century, Thomas de Cuckney built a castle. Excavations on the site in the 1950s found the remains of hundreds of skeletons though it is unlikely that they are from the days of the Dark Ages. More recent research has dated the remains to the 7th century and the Battle of Heathfield between Edwin of Northumbria and Penda of Mercia.

Blue Barn Farm lies very much off the beaten track near the village of *Langwith* just to the west of Cuckney. Following the ring farm system the farmhouse lies at the heart of the land that it farms and so it is isolated. From the charming farmhouse, built in 1900, June Ibbotson offers warm and friendly bed and breakfast accommodation. Blue Barn Cottage, a four bedroom self-catering cottage, is also available for those who wish to look after themselves in this delightful spot. *Blue Barn Farm, Langwith, Mansfield, Nottinghamshire NG20 9JD Tel: 01623 742248*

Boon Hills Farm, in a beautiful, isolated position, lies a quarter of a mile down its own dedicated lane off the east road out of *Nether Langwith* in the direction of Cuckney. This working arable and beef farm of 160 acres has been occupied by the Palmers for 20 years and, from the large, attractive farmhouse, Lesley Palmer also offers excellent bed and breakfast accommodation. The house has three comfortable guest bedrooms, a guests' lounge with tea and coffee making facilities and television, and, though there is no evening meal, the large breakfast will really set guests up for the day. Surrounded by a large, well established garden, where Lesley is happy to serve guests pots of tea while they take in the superb views over the farmland, Boon Hills Farmhouse is a lovely place to

Boon Hills Farm

stay, where all are made welcome. *Boon Hills Farm, Nether Langwith, Mansfield, Nottinghamshire NG20 9JQ Tel: 01623 743862*

CHAPTER FOUR
Sherwood Forest

Medieval Knight, Sherwood Forest

Chapter 4 - Area Covered

*For precise location of places please refer to the colour
maps found at the rear of the book.*

● East Retford

● Worksop

● Mansfield
Woodhouse

● Mansfield

NOTTINGHAMSHIRE

● Sutton in Ashfield

Newark
on Trent ●

● Kirkby in Ashfield

● Hucknall

● Arnold

● NOTTINGHAM

● Beeston

4
Sherwood Forest

Introduction

Sherwood Forest is known to old and young alike, all over the world, thanks to the tales of Robin Hood and the various stories, films, and, television series made about this legendary hero of the people. Sherwood, the shire wood of Nottinghamshire, was once part of a great mass of forest land which covered much of central England; stretching from Nottingham in the south to Worksop in the north and from the Peak District to the Trent Valley in the east.

It was likely that William the Conqueror, during his reign, designated Sherwood a royal forest. An administrative term for the private hunting ground of the king, the land was not only thickly wooded but also included areas of rough heathland as well as arable land, meadow land, small towns, and villages. The Norman kings were passionate about their hunting and, to guard their royal forests, there were a set of rigidly upheld laws, to conserve the game (known as the venison) and vegetation (known as the vert). No one, even those with a private estate within the royal forest, was allowed to kill or hunt protected animals, graze domestic animals in the forest, fell trees, or make clearings within the boundaries without the express permission of the king or one of his chief foresters. It is little wonder then, that with such strict rules imposed upon them, that the people turned to the likes of Robin Hood and others who defied the laws and lived off the king's deer. Though villagers were severely punished for breaking the forest law, the Norman kings were well known for frequently offering exemptions from the rule to favoured noblemen as well as local monastic houses.

It was not until the Tudor and Stuart monarchs came to the throne in the 16th century that things began to change and the laws relaxed. Less obsessed with hunting than their predecessors, the kings granted permission for the felling of trees and the clearing of land for agricultural purposes and so the landscape of the forest began to change. Eventually, the royal forest was broken up and the land given to various aristocratic families in the area. In particular are the four great private estates in the northern part of the forest, Rufford, Welbeck, Clumber, and Thoresby, which became known as The Dukeries.

The great oaks of the forest were felled in their thousands for shipbuilding and also to fuel the iron industry. Later, in the 19th century, the decline of the forest areas increased with the sinking of mines in the forest. Starting on the southern and western fringes of Sherwood Forest gradually the collieries moved inwards turning once small rural communities into mining villages. The peak of destruction of the wooded areas was reached during World War I. Where, once the forest covered a large part of the county, only a few pockets of wood and heathland remained, chiefly the area around Edwinstowe.

Following World War I, the Forestry Commission was set up to replenish the depleted stocks of wood and a programme of planting began. Since World War II, when the forest areas were used again, there has been a great change in the fortunes of Sherwood. Whilst, conifers were the first trees to be planted, they have now reached maturity and the Forestry Commission which still manages much of the land has also reintroduced the traditional deciduous tress.

Edwinstowe

Lying at the heart of Sherwood Forest, the life of the village is still dominated by the forest, as it has been since the 7th century. Edwin, King of Northumbria, who gave the village its name, died in the Battle of Hatfield in 632 and the village is said to have grown up around the church which was built on the spot where he was slain. In 1912, a cross was erected to mark his grave by the Duke of Portland. From then on until the time of the Domesday Survey, Edwinstowe remained small. Following the Norman Conquest, the village found itself within the boundaries of the Royal Hunting Forest of Sherwood and it became subject to the laws of the forest. Dating from the 12th century, the **Church of St Mary** was the first stone building in Edwinstowe and legend has it that it was here that the marriage took place between Robin Hood and Maid Marian.

A little way up the road leading northwards out of Edwinstowe is the **Sherwood Forest Visitor Centre**. Sherwood, the Shire Wood, was once a great woodland mass, stretching from Nottingham to Worksop. Although only relatively small pockets of the original forest remain today, it is still possible to become lost amongst the trees, both figuratively and literally! Whether or not Robin and his Merry Men ever did frolic in the greenshawe is, however, debatable. Arguments still rage as to which particular historical figure gave rise to the legend of the famous outlaw. Records from the 12th century suggest a number of possible candidates, including the Earl of Huntingdon.

The Major Oak, Sherwood Forest

During the 15th century, several references to the outlaw can be found in the writings of two Scottish historians and, in 1521, a third Scotsman, John Major, wrote "About the time of King Richard I, according to my estimate the famous English robbers Robert Hood and Little John were lurking in their woods, preying on the goods of the wealthy." However, none of the historians gave any clues as to the sources of their writings. By the 16th century, there were two conflicting stories emerging as to the birthplace of Robin, one suggesting Kirklees whilst the other suggested Locksley.

Tracing the stories of Robin Hood is a difficult task as the tales, which have been told for over 600 years, were told rather than written as few local people could read and write. One of the earliest known stories of the outlaw's exploits can be found on a piece of parchment which dates from the mid-15th century but it was not until William Caxton set up his printing press in London in 1477 that cheaper books could be produced. From then on, the story of Robin Hood, his merry band of men, Guy of Gisbourne, and the wicked Sheriff of Nottingham has been popular and the any book of their deeds a best seller.

Undeterred by the vague foundations upon which the legend is built, visitors still flock to see the great hollow tree which the outlaws purportedly used as a meeting place and as a cache for their supplies. The **Major Oak** which is located about 10 minutes walk along the main track in the heart of the forest. This huge tree, which is not so much tall as broad, with its massive wooden crutches and supportive iron corsets presents a rather forlorn sight. There is no denying that it is at least 500 years old, and some sources would claim it to be more than double that figure. Yet despite its appearance, the tree is still alive thanks to careful preservation. Recent tests have established that some parts of the tree have successfully taken to grafting and one hopes that at some stage a whole colony of minor oaks may be produced.

The visitor centre also houses a display of characters from the Robin Hood stories, with appropriate scenes of merry making. This theme has been more successfully translated to the city of Nottingham in the Tales of Robin Hood exhibition, and the children certainly enjoy it.

The Dukeries Hotel

The Dukeries Hotel was built in 1890 to accommodate tourists arriving by the newly built railway. The original building had an enormous ballroom which unfortunately burned down in 1929. An outstanding property, it is ideal for the tourist to use as a base or as a stopover for the traveller. Four of the six bedrooms have en-suite facilities, one bedroom having a four-poster and another a waterbed.

The Dukeries is open everyday and meals are served every lunchtime and Wednesday to Saturday evenings. The menu offers three course meals on an à la carte basis and there should be something to satisfy all tastes. Lighter meals and snacks are available and there is a children's menu too. Excellent Mansfield ales and a full complement of wines and spirits are served in the comfortable bars. *The Dukeries Hotel, Edwinstowe, Nottinghamshire NG21 9HS Tel: 01623 823584*

Those looking for a memento of their visit to Sherwood Forest should make a point of finding **Robin's Den** in the heart of the historic village of Edwinstowe. Located at 17 High Street, this de-

Robin's Den

lightful gift shop is stocked with a tremendous selection of Robin Hood souvenirs, Nottingham lace, quality cards, and other gift ideas. Proprietor Winona Turvill has assembled an impressive range of cards to mark every occasion, including those by local artists, as well as well-known makes from around the country. She also specialises in articles made from the famous local Nottingham lace, including tablecloths, cushion covers, curtains, and smaller items to suit every pocket. There is also a charming range of hand-trimmed baby accessories which are made by Winona's older daughter, Justine. The wide variety of Robin Hood mementos on offer includes hats and tea towels and there is also a good selection of traditional hand-painted canalware and framed bathroom pictures which are individually designed and made locally.

Another impressive attraction in Edwinstowe is the **Sherwood Forest Amusement Park** which can be found to the north of the A6075 Mansfield to Ollerton road. This family-run funfair contains a variety of popular fairground rides, including dodgems, a ghost train, and a giant Astroglide. Open daily, 10.00 to dusk between mid-March and mid-October; admission free. *Robin's Den, 17 High Street, Edwinstowe, Nottinghamshire NG21 9QP Tel: 01623 824117*

Not far from Edwinstowe, off the A6075, is the ***Sherwood Forest Farm Park***, a naturalist and animal lover's delight. Enjoying a peaceful setting in a secluded valley on the edge of Sherwood Forest, the Farm Park boasts no fewer than 30 rare and threatened species of farm animal and is beautifully laid out, with ornamental ponds and three wildfowl lakes. A peaceful spot to relax can be found by visitors even on the busiest of days. The pets corner and the aviary of exotic birds is always a delight. There is so much to see

Sherwood Forest Farm Park

and do here that it is every bit a fun day out for the adults as for the younger family members. Youngsters will appreciate the adventure playground and everyone can enjoy playing spot the baby wallabies in their mums' pouches, while wandering round the scenic farmland. With a tearoom, gift shop, picnic area, and much more besides, there is too much to list here that visitors are best advised to come and see for themselves. Ring for details of special events. *Sherwood Forest Farm Park, Lamb Pens Farm, Edwinstowe, Nottinghamshire NG21 9HL Tel: 01623 823558*

South of Edwinstowe

Rainworth   *Map 3 ref C5*
6 miles S of Edwinstowe on the A617
Pronounced Renoth locally, this is a mining village and its development is solely due to the now closed pits. There are, however, two

very different places of interest within the village. **Rainworth Water**, a series of lakes and streams, which attracts walkers, naturalists, and fishermen, is also the site of a bird sanctuary founded by the naturalist Joseph Whitaker.

Rainworth's other claim to fame is its fish and chip shop which found itself on the front pages of the national newspapers in the early 1980s as the place where the Black Panther was caught. A local shopkeeper had noticed a man loitering in the area and had contacted the police who kept a watch for the suspicious man on the main street of the village. Suddenly realising that he was being followed, the suspect began shooting at the police, injuring one, but the customers in the chip shop, seeing what was going on, caught the man. Though at the time the police did not know the identity of the gunman he later turned out to be the notorious Black Panther and was convicted of murder in the West Midlands.

Blidworth   *Map 3 ref C5*
7 miles S of Edwinstowe on the B6020

A small forest village which changed greatly with the opening of a colliery in the 1920s, Blidworth may indeed change again as the pits closed in the late 1980s. As well as a having a mixture of 1930s miners' homes and early stone cottages, there is also a particularly attractive church. Dating back to 1739, the **Church of St Mary of the Purification** has some interesting items, including Continental glass and Jacobean panelling. A rather touching monument in the church is one dedicated to a forest ranger called Thomas Leake, who died there in 1598. The stone memorial has some splendid carvings of stags and dogs, denoting his role as a Sherwood Ranger.

The village also has many associations with the legend of Robin Hood. Maid Marian is thought to have lived here before her marriage to the outlaw; at Fountaindale are the remains of **Friar Tuck's Well** and, nearby, the site of his home where his fight with Robin is said to have taken place; and, finally, Will Scarlett is reputedly buried in St Mary's churchyard.

Near the village there are two Forestry Commission areas of woodland which both offer the opportunity for walks and picnics: **Blidworth Bottoms** and **Haywood Oaks**, where some of the largest oak trees in Sherwood can be found.

Ravenshead   *Map 3 ref B5*
8 miles S of Edwinstowe on the A60

Although the name Ravenshead appears in the Domesday Book, the village of Ravenshead is relatively new and dates from 1966 when the three hamlets of Fishpool, Larch Farm, and Kighill merged. Situated by the side of the main road is the **Bessie Shepherd Stone** which marks the spot where, in 1817, Bessie was murdered as she walked from Mansfield to Papplewick.

Longdale Lane Rural Craft Centre was established in the 1970s and it is the oldest such centre in the country. A re-creation of a 19th-century village, complete with flagstones and Victorian street lamps, behind the decorative, period shop fronts a whole host of professional artists can be seen making both traditional and modern objects.

North of Edwinstowe

Meden Vale
3 miles NW of Edwinstowe off the A616

Map 1 ref C4

Formerly called Welbeck Colliery Village, the name, which comes from the nerby River Meden, was changed in 1975. The colliery was originally sunk in 1913 and the village grew up around the pit in the 1920s when miners moved into the area from the north of England and Scotland. Now no longer worked, the spoil heaps around the pit have been landscaped and provide a habitat for local wildlife and trees and bulbs have been planted.

Shireoaks
10 miles NW of Edwinstowe off the A57

Map 1 ref B2

This old and very attractive village takes its name from an ancient oak tree which stood here overlooking the three shires of Yorkshire, Derbyshire, and Nottinghamshire. Once a rural, forest village, Shireoaks, like so many others in the area, became a mining village when a pit was sunk in the 1850s. Fortunately, though, agricultural has not been forgotten here and, as well as being chiefly concerned with arable farming, one farm also breeds prize winning Friesian cattle.

Although the village church is neither ancient nor of any particular note architecturally, it does has several interesting connections for so small a building. The foundation stone was laid in 1861 by the Prince of Wales (later Edward VII) and WE Gladstone, then Chancellor of the Exchequer, came to dedicate the east windows.

Clumber Park
5 miles N of Edwinstowe off the A614

Map 1 ref C3

As country estates go, Clumber Park is relatively new as it only dates from 1707 when the 3rd Duke of Newcastle was granted permission to enclose part of the Forest of Sherwood as a hunting ground for Queen Anne. The building of **Clumber House** began in 1760 though it was much altered in the early 19th century. After a devastating fire in 1879, the house was rebuilt in an Italianate style but, due to vast expense of the up keep of such a mansion, Clumber House was demolished in 1938 and all that remains today are the foundations.

However, any sense of disappointment is quickly dispelled by the charm of the buildings that remain in this lovely setting. The estate houses with their high pitched gables and massive chimneys are most impressive. The red-brick stables are particularly fine as they are surmounted by a clocktower crowned by a domed cupola. The inset clock in the tower dates back to 1763 and the stables now house the café and visitor centre.

However, by far the most striking building on the estate is the **Church of St Mary the Virgin**, built GF Bodley in the late 19th century. Commissioned by the 7th Duke of Newcastle, a fervent Anglo-Catholic, no expense was spared and the church has many elaborate features including its wonderful stone and woodwork.

The park is owned by the National Trust and attracts many visitors, especially throughout the summer when special events are arranged. The man-made lake is particularly lovely and is crossed by a fine classical bridge. Another impressive feature is the entrance to the park through the Apleyhead Gate. Known as the **Duke's Drive** and stretching for a distance of two miles, it is now established as the longest avenue of limes in Europe and contains some 1296 trees.

Perlethorpe   *Map 1 ref C3*
5 miles NE of Edwinstowe off the B6387

Situated in the valley of the River Meden, Perlethorpe also lies on the estate of **Thoresby Hall**. The first hall was built in the late 17th century for the Earl of Kingston but this was destroyed in 1745 and replaced by a Palladian-style mansion. The hall seen today is a Victorian mansion built by Anthony Salvin in 1864 for the Pierrepont family and it is surrounded by the largest park in the county situated in Sherwood Forest. Now in private hands, Thoresby Hall is not open to the public.

The village church, which was completed in 1876, was also built by Salvin at the same as he was working on the hall. At the beginning of the 20th century Lady Manvers would take a keen interest in the welfare of the village children and ask to be informed of any which did not attend Sunday school. She would the visit them and, if the child was sick, ensure that hot soup was delivered to the child until they were well again.

Bothamsall
Map 1 ref C3
5 miles NE of Edwinstowe off the B6387

Close to Bothamsall the two rivers, the Meden and the Maun, finally merge to become the River Idle. This pretty village with its twisting lane has a pleasant church that looks much older than its 150 years. There was a church on this site originally which dated back to the 14th century, but the only remaining relics are a few monuments and the font.

A road to the west of the village leads up to **Castle Hill** where a ruined outer wall of a castle and an artificial motte formed part of the local defences. No other evidence points to a larger fortification and, as no records exist of a defence to protect this strategic crossing point, the date of the castle can only be guessed to be around the 12th century. However, the views from the hill top are well worth the climb and not only can the plantations which form the Clumber and Thoresby estates be seen but also the neo-Georgian house, **Lound Hall**, which was built in 1937 at nearby **Haughton**. Now open to the public as the **National Mining Museum**, the hall is also a training centre.

The museum, which lies close to one of the most modern pits in the country, has a whole range of exhibits which illustrate the development of the coal industry in Great Britain. Inside, the displays include early Davy safety lamps, tools, equipment, old documents, and photographs whilst, outside, are a whole range of larger exhibits including pumping and winding gear, an underground canal boat, and coalface machinery.

Thaymar Dairy Ice Cream, produced at Haughton Park Farm near Bothamsall, is easy to find as it lies just a short distance from the A1. A most attractive and well-kept farm, it offers a real treat to the traveller. The ice cream produced by Thelma Cheetham is truly superb. Real home-produced ice cream made only with the best natural ingredients. The variety is enormous and ingredients come from as far afield as Italy and Mauritius. An exceptional treat for warm summer days or indeed desert, flavourings such as Marsala, rum and raisin, coconut, caramel hazelnut, Gaelic coffee, peaches and cream, Caribbean fruit, kiwi, and pure Mediterranean lemon or tangy orange sorbets are enough to compliment the most formal of dinner parties. Other flavours available range from vanilla through to blackberry.

Now such a successful wholesaler to restaurants and commercial premises covering a wide area, all are welcome to call into the farm and sample these delicious treats. The tea room situated in an attractive farm cottage, is spotlessly clean and offers visitors a large selection of snacks ranging from freshly made sandwiches to jacket potatoes with a variety of tempting fillings. Extra special home-made gateaux and dairy deserts offer visitors the opportunity for further indulgence. The young visitor is also able to enjoy the play

Thaymar Dairy Ice Cream

slide and the close proximity of farm animals. The farm has been in the Cheetham family since 1923 and is mainly a dairy farm supporting 80 pedigree Friesians. Anyone calling at the farm will surely be unable to walk away without resisting the temptation to purchase some of these mouthwatering desserts. *Thaymar Dairy Ice Cream, Haughton Park Farm, near Bothamsall, Nottinghamshire DN22 8DB Tel: 01623 860320*

East Markham   Map 2 ref D3
7 miles NE of Edwinstowe off the A57
The name of the village suggests that it lay on a boundary and, indeed, East Markham lies on a ridge of high land between the Rivers Idle and Trent. In medieval times the prefix East was added to distinguish the village from West Markham and, at one time, the village was referred to as Great Markham. Perhaps suggesting that

it had out grown its sister. Still very much a farming community, though unusually the crops here are fruit, East Markham at one time was a thriving market centre. It was not taken over by a growing neighbouring town but East Markham lost its prominence in this field due to the plague which struck here in 1609. The vicar of the time kept a record of all those in the parish who succumbed to the disease though the last entry, of his own death, is written in another hand.

CHAPTER FIVE
Rural Nottinghamshire

Southwell Minster

Chapter 5 - Area Covered

*For precise location of places please refer to the colour
maps found at the rear of the book.*

● East Retford

● Worksop

● Mansfield
Woodhouse

● Mansfield

NOTTINGHAMSHIRE

● Sutton in Ashfield

Newark
on Trent ●

● Kirkby in Ashfield

● Hucknall

● Arnold

● NOTTINGHAM

● Beeston

5
Rural Nottinghamshire

Introduction

This area of Nottinghamshire, through which the River Trent flows, is a maze of country lanes and ancient villages. Only the southern area was ever part of the Royal Hunting Forest of Sherwood and, this flat and fertile land, has been farmed for centuries. The village of Laxton, in the heart of the county, has throughout the years managed to maintain the medieval open field system of farming despite the advance in farming methods over this time. Flooding has, however, been a problem over the years as the River Trent meanders through the fields.

At the centre of rural Nottinghamshire is the town of Southwell which is sheltered from the severest of weathers by the surrounding small hills. Dominated by its Minster, Southwell is little more than a village but it has some interesting, ancient buildings which include the inn where Charles I spent his last night of freedom. The town is also home to the Bramley apple and the local dish, Southwell Galette, is well worth tasting.

Further north, on the medieval boundaries of Sherwood Forest, lies Ollerton, the only other town in this area. The old town looks very much as it did centuries ago though the discovery of coal in the vicinity in the 19th century has lead to the development of colliery village of New Ollerton.

Southwell

An elegant market town, Southwell also boasts a fine *Cathedral*, which may sound implausible to the uninitiated, but the lovely 12th-century *Minster* was elevated to the status of cathedral in 1884, when the new Diocese of Southwell was created. This has given rise to the building often being referred to as the village cathedral. The two west towers, with their pyramidal roofs, make a striking landmark as they stand proud, dominating the cathedral green. Inside, the choir screen is quite stunning, bearing no less than 200 human carvings, and the eagle lectern, which stands in the choir, was salvaged from the lake at Newstead Abbey in 1750. It had been thrown there by the monks to protect it from the looting that occurred during the Dissolution and was presented to the minster in 1805. The chapter house also has some beautiful carvings which date from the 13th century.

To the south of the minster can be found the ruins of the palace of the archbishops of York which dated from the 14th and 15th centuries. Parts of the old palace, closest to the minster's south doorway, have been incorporated into the present **Bishop's Palace**.

Southwell itself has many fine buildings and a wealth of fascinating places to discover. Among these are the Prebendal houses where the secular canons resided, sequestered alleyways, and charming coaching inns like the **Saracen's Head** where Charles I spent his last hours of freedom before his final surrender. At the time of the king's final visit the inn was called the King's Head but the name of this wonderful 16th-century inn was changed after Charles's execution.

Burgage Manor

The young Lord Byron stayed at **Burgage Manor**, a fine Regency house, with his mother between 1803 and 1807 whilst on holiday from Harrow and Cambridge. He was a member of the local theatrical group and it was his friends in the town who convinced him to publish his first set of poems. One of his earlier collections, *Hours of Idleness*, was published by Ridges of Newark and was to bring him great acclaim.

Southwell can also be credited as the birthplace of the Bramley apple. The story goes that in the early 19th century, two ladies planted some apple pips in their cottage garden in the nearby village of Easthorpe. Nature took its course and one of the seedlings grew into a tree. By this time, Matthew Bramley owned the cottage and the quality of the tree's fruit began to excite public interest.

Mr Henry Merryweather, a local nurseryman, persuaded Bramley to let him take a cutting, which he consequently propagated with enormous success. Permission had been granted on the condition that the apples took Mr Bramley's name and not the two ladies'! Whilst in the town visitors should look out for Southwell Galette, a scrumptious pastry confection of hazelnuts, sultanas, and, of course, Bramley apples.

The now disused railway line from Southwell to Mansfield, which was first opened to trains in 1871, is now an attractive and comfortable footpath known as the *Farnsfield to Southwell Trail*. As well as the varied plant and wildlife that can be found along the 4 1/2 mile walk, there is also plenty of industrial archaeological interest including the *Farnsfield Waterworks* of 1910, a late 18th-century cotton mill, and *Greet Lily Mill*, a corn mill on the banks of the River Greet.

Norwood Park is the only one of the four original parks around Southwell which remains today. The property of the Archbishops of York, the park remained in the possession of the Church until 1778 and, though a house was built here in Cromwell's day, the present building dates from 1763. Open to visitors during the summer months, the house has a very lived in feel and, as well as many 17th- and 18th-century family portraits, there is also a fine collection of china.

The surrounding parkland was laid out in the 18th century at the same time as the ice house and temple were built and the lime avenue planted. However, the park is much older and it is believed that some of the fishponds received a mention in the Domesday Book.

The *Admiral Rodney Hotel*, on one of the main streets, started life as The White Lyon but, in 1781, it was renamed after Admiral Rodney's famous battle at Cape St Vincent. This attractive building dates back to the early 18th century and, inside, one of the most prominent features are the ceiling beams which came from HMS Rodney. In 1961, when the hotel was being renewed, a beam from the bell ringing gallery in the minster was added and, during renovation work in 1985, a medieval well was discovered. The well is now exposed to the public and it makes an interesting and unusual focal point in the bar area. Writing found on some of the walls relates to the well and also to other historical facts regarding the premises.

Admiral Rodney Hotel

This was, when first built, a coaching inn and the front door, up to which the stage coaches and carriages drew, is now at the back of the building. The old carriageway is now home to a conservatory but the old features are clearly visible. As with many old buildings, the Admiral Rodney Hotel has its own ghost, in this case there are actually two. The first is Charlie, an old solider who is believed to have hanged himself in the disused ballroom during World War I when the hotel was being used as a hospital. The second is a lady, no one knows who, dressed as a nanny.

Today, the Admiral Rodney Hotel carries on the tradition of offering refreshment and shelter to travellers. An interesting and varied menu is served, at lunchtimes only, and six traditional ales are always available. Accommodation is offered in five comfortable bedrooms with a further four en-suite family rooms being planned. *Admiral Rodney Hotel, King Street, Southwell, Nottinghamshire NG25 0EH Tel: 01636 812292*

South and East of Southwell

Oxton   *Map 3 ref C5*
4 miles SW of Southwell on the B6386

An ancient Saxon settlement lying on the edge of Sherwood Forest, Oxton was recorded in the Domesday Book. The uncovering of **Oldox Camp**, one of the largest Iron Age hill forts in Nottinghamshire, to the north of the village suggests that this was the original site of Oxton. Extending over some 3 acres, the fort is surrounded by a single ditch and bank, except at the entrance to the fort where the defences are doubled.

The village **Church of St Peter and St Paul** has its foundations in Saxon times though the chancel is Norman and the nave and tower date from the 14th century. In 1986, the work to add two more church bells, bringing the total to six, was finished; the oldest bell, which is still very much in use, dates from 1638.

The Sherbrooke family have been the lords of the manor since the 16th century and Oxton still retains the feel of an estate village even though the hall was demolished in 1957. In one farmyard can be found the tomb of Robert Sherbrooke, who died in the early 18th century. This unusual position for a burial was probably chosen as this farmyard is believed to have been a resting place of the Quakers as well as the site of their meeting house.

Calverton   *Map 3 ref C6*
6 miles SW of Southwell off the B6386

The charming cottages in this industrial village date back to the early 19th century and they were the homes of framework knitters. Carefully restored by the Nottinghamshire Building Preservation Trust, the cottages originally formed three sides of a rectangle, though one side is now missing. Unusually, the large windows which provided the light for the knitters are found on the ground floor where, elsewhere, they are usually on an upper storey.

Framework knitting was the main industry of the village, and of many others, at that time. The stocking knitting frame was invented in nearby Woodborough by William Lee in 1589. Born in Calverton, Lee's wooden frame so revolutionised the stocking industry that he attempted to seek patronage from Elizabeth I. Unfortunately, the wind was taken out of his sails as she refused to grant a patent for something that would mean great job losses for her loyal subjects! Little is known of William Lee though there is no doubt of him having invented the knitting frame. There is also no information which supports romantic suggestions that Lee wanted to impress his wife or to outdo a woman knitter.

After being refused a patent by Elizabeth I, Lee travelled to France and gained the promise of support from Henry of Navarre. Unfortunately, Henry was assassinated before any promises were made good and it is believed that Lee died in Paris in 1610. Lee's brother, James, brought the frame back to London where the hosiery industry first developed before it settled in the Midlands later in the 17th century. The *Calverton Folk Museum* (open by appointment) houses many items particular to the hosiery industry as well as some period furnishings.

Also at Calverton is *Painters' Paradise*, a series of gardens that have been designed with the artist in mind. Covering some 38 acres, the gardens, which have elements based on Monet's garden at Giverny, include woodlands, meadows, butterfly gardens, and a special disabled garden with raised flower beds. Old farming implements are used as props and there are several gazebos so that people can paint in comfort.

Epperstone   Map 4 ref C6
4 miles SW of Southwell off the A6097
Though this attractive village, protected by a conservation order, has no particularly noteworthy buildings or monuments, Epperstone does have a pleasant and unspoilt feel as well as some elegant Georgian and Victorian houses and some earlier cottages.

The Lofthouse

The Lofthouse is a charming self-catering cottage found on Criftin Farm in the village and just off the B6386 Newark to Southwell road. A 17th-century granary conversion, the cottage has been beautifully decorated and furnished to provide wonderful accommodation in two twin bedded rooms each with their own private bathroom. Along with a wonderful, beamed lounge and a large fully equipped kitchen, this is the perfect place to make a holiday base.

Criftin Farm is owned and run by Jenny Esam and her family and has been farmed by the same family for five generations. In these pleasant surroundings, with walks in the woods at the back of the farm, guests at The Lofthouse can enjoy the countryside, the outdoor heated swimming pool, and games room and can be sure that Jenny will ensure that everything guests need for a super holiday is provided. *The Lofthouse, Criftin Farm, Epperstone, Nottinghamshire NG14 6AT Tel: 0115 9652039*

Lowdham   Map 4 ref C6
5 miles S of Southwell on the A6097
Known locally as the village which ran away from the church, Lowdham acquired this unusual nickname after the construction of a dual carriageway was built in the 1930s. Dividing the village in two, the carriageway left the church on one side with much of the rest of the village on the other.

Founded in the late 12th century, the **Church of St Mary the Virgin** houses an effigy of Sir Jon de Ludham, a knight whose son fought with Edward III at the Battle of Crecy. Nearby, is the Old Hall which dates back, in part, to Elizabethan times and was once called Broughton Hall.

Lambley   Map 3 ref C6
7 miles SW of Southwell off the A612
As its name suggests, Lambley was the place where lambs were reared and the fields around the village are still home to grazing sheep and lambs. Though close to both Southwell and Nottingham, Lambley's air of rural peace and tranquillity are gained from its position, at the bottom of a valley formed by the branches of the Cocker Beck, a tributary of the River Trent.

An ancient settlement, after the Norman Conquest the manor of Lambley was granted to the Cromwell family and, in 1394, Lord Ralph Cromwell was born in the village. Lord Cromwell went on to become Lord Treasurer of England in the time of Henry VI and he also has the distinction of presenting the first budget to Parliament. Though he gained great wealth, Lord Cromwell did not forget his birthplace and, in his will, he made provision for the rebuilding of the village church. After his death, the manor fell into disrepair and today the site on which the house stood is known as the Pingle.

Right up until the early 19th century, Lambley remained very much a rural community but then the framework knitting industry took over. Though many of the typical long windows have either been altered or bricked up, the cottages where the knitters worked long, hard hours can still be seen.

Floralands Garden Centre began in 1882, when the grandfather of the present managing director started a market garden and horticulture business. Since then the establishment has expanded immensely and the garden centre now covers a total of 28 acres, with eight acres given over to the centre, two acres to Playworld, and the rest is still used for farming.

Floralands Garden Centre

Although Floralands contains everything the gardener could possibly wish for or want for their garden, the garden centre specializes in large trees and shrubs, some of which are imported from Italy. There is also a large area given specifically to clematis, in all the different varieties. As well as plants, of all shape, colour, and size, Floralands is also renowned for its fine selection of garden furniture. However, perhaps the centre's most interesting feature is a giant Christmas Cacti: planted in 1968 and with over 600 grafts, this amazing plant now produces a staggering 50,000 blooms a year - and it is still growing.

For the experienced and amateur gardener alike, this is a wonderful place to come to, the staff are both informed and helpful and are on hand to offer advice should any be required. For the rest of the family, there is a small aviary and a number of franchises are also at the centre selling a number of garden and outdoor related items and services. The cosy tea room seats about 30 and offers often much welcomed refreshments and a sit down. For the children there is **Playworld**, a premier tourist attraction in the county and a wonderful safe play area for youngsters. Catering for children of all ages, there are imaginative slides and swings and, perhaps most popular of all, there is a real fire engine for them to clamber over. *Floralands Garden Centre and Playworld, Catfoot Lane, Lambley, Nottingham NG4 4QL Tel: 0115 967 0487*

Burton Joyce
Map 3 ref C6

8 miles SW of Southwell on the A612
Originally known simply as Burton, this village on the banks of the River Trent gained the second half of its name when Jorz was added after the name of the key landowning family in the area. Much later, the village came into the hands of the Earls of Carnarvon and the Carnarvon Reading Room is named after the 5th Earl, who is better known as the discoverer of the Tomb of Tutankhamen.

Shelford
Map 3 ref C6

8 miles S of Southwell off the A6097
The name Shelford means the place of the shallow ford and, presumably, there was once a ford across the River Trent which flows close to the village. Though now a quiet and tranquil place, in the winter of 1644 Shelford was the site of a particularly fierce battle. Royalist soldiers, taking shelter in the church tower, were smoked out by the Parliamentarian army who set fire to straw at the tower's base. During the same weekend a whole garrison of soldiers, some 200 men, were slaughtered by Cromwell's men at the manor house which was subsequently burnt to the ground.

East Bridgford
Map 3 ref B6

7 miles S of Southwell off the A6097
The village is situated on a ridge overlooking a crossing of the River Trent and the edge of Sherwood Forest beyond. The village **Church of St Peter** certainly dates from the 9th century as it is known to have been plundered by the Danes when they came up the river to Nottingham. Rebuilt since then it remains the centre of life in the village and, since the 15th century, has had strong associations with St Magdalen College, Oxford.

From the early 18th century until 1936 gypsum has been extensively mined in the village and the Satin Spar, as it was known, was of such a fine quality that is was exported to North America. At one time there were several craftsmen in the village making orna-ments from the spar and examples of their work have been exhib-ited in London.

Gunthorpe

Map 3 ref C6

6 miles S of Southwell off the A6097

This small, old village owes its existence to the ford here across the River Trent. During the 1st century the Romans used the ford when travelling between their fort at Margidunum in the east to the lead mines of Derbyshire. It was also here that the famous warrior Queen Boadicea defeated a Roman legion in a fierce battle.

Mentioned in the Domesday Book, William the Conqueror granted the manor of Gunthorpe, along with others in the area, to one of his faithful noblemen, Roger de Busli.

The Unicorn Hotel is a large, old 17th-century coaching inn which stands in a picturesque setting on the banks of the River Trent. A welcome haven for tourists and businessmen alike, the hotel continues the tradition of providing accommodation and re-freshment to weary travellers. Though the warmth of welcome has not changed over the years, the standard of the hospitality has - this is one of the better hotels in the area.

The Unicorn Hotel

Tastefully furnished and decorated, the hotel's refurbishment has captured the atmosphere and style of days gone by; wood panelled rooms, low beams, and an array of memorabilia all add to the air of tradition and permanence. As well as offering a fine selection of real ales, an extensive and varied menu is served in the attractive oak panelled restaurant which overlooks the river. For those look-ing for overnight accommodation there are 16 superbly decorated, comfortable en-suite bedrooms which will guarantee a good night's rest. Special weekend and family rates apply. *The Unicorn Hotel, Gunthorpe Bridge, Gunthorpe, Nottinghamshire NG14 7FB Tel: 0115 966 3612*

Thurgaton   *Map 3 ref B6*
3 miles S of Southwell off the A612

This picturesque village is one of the most ancient settlements in Nottinghamshire and its name comes from the old Norse name Thorgeirr. Following the Norman Conquest, William granted the manor of Thurgaton, along with 34 others in Nottinghamshire, to Walter d'Ayncourt. It was Walter's second son, Roger, who, in the mid-12th century, founded **Thurgaton Priory** for the Augustinian order. Originally built to the size of Southwell Minster, it is said that one of the Black Canons still haunts the priory grounds.

In 1538, Henry VIII closed the priory, granting the buildings to William Cooper and the land to Trinity College, Cambridge. The priory church fell into disrepair, with many of the villagers making use of the stone and timber in their own houses, and it was not until 1854 that the church was restored by the Milward family. Some of the priory's other stone buildings were replaced by a Georgian house and, in 1884, when the diocese of Southwell was founded the bishop lived at the priory. It is now owned by Boots plc, who have their research centre here.

Finally, Thurgaton also a very pleasant cricket ground which is overlooked by both the church and the priory. Though not a large place the village can still turn out a couple of teams and regularly places host to matches with other villages.

Bleasby   *Map 3 ref D6*
3 miles S of Southwell off the A612

This attractive village, near to the River Trent, offers a full range of leisure pursuits both from the river bank and on the water itself. The village is a real blend of the old and new. The oldest is the 14th-century farmhouse, Manor Farm, which also has a very fine 18th-century square **Dovecote**. Built of brick and with a tiled roof, the dovecote has, halfway up, a projecting brick ledge to prevent rats from getting into the cote through the flight holes.

The founder of the Salvation Army, Sir William Booth, spent some years in the village as a young boy when his family lived at Old Farm. Booth's sister, Mary, was baptised in the village Church of St Mary the Virgin.

Fiskerton
Map 4 ref D6

3 miles SE of Southwell off the A612

The village lies on the banks of the River Trent, which played an important part in the prosperity of Fiskerton during the 19th century. Not only was Fiskerton a hive of activity with a lace factory and a firm making stove polish, blackening, and ink but it was also busy with river traffic and there were warehouses and wharves along the banks.

Fiskerton was also the place where the troops coming from Southwell crossed the River Trent in 1487 on their way to the final battle of the Wars of the Roses at East Stoke. Today, the village is much more peaceful; a walk along the riverbank provides the opportunity to see a heron or even a kingfisher whilst Southwell racecourse lies on the village border.

Farndon
Map 4 ref D5

4 miles SE of Southwell off the A46

There has been a settlement here since Roman times when the village's name was Farendune, meaning the place in the bracken on the bank. The church of St Peter, situated in the oldest part of the village, has both Saxon and Norman details.

During the 1930s, when the aerodromes at Syerston and Newton were under construction, sand and gravel were needed for the building of the runways. Both were taken from the banks of the River Trent here and, today, the pits which the excavations made, have been transformed into a lovely marina.

Rolleston
Map 4 ref D5

3 miles E of Southwell off the A617

By all appearances Rolleston is a typical, pleasant Nottinghamshire village which happens to have a particularly fine church. However, at the time of the Domesday Survey, the village was recorded as having at least three manors. Evidence for these manors is almost nonexistant today, but it is known that the Neville manor existed in the late 13th century. ***Holy Trinity Church*** is certainly one of the county's finest churches and it is also the home of a great treasure: a portion of the original paper register covering the years 1584 to 1615. An interesting and historic document completed by the vicar of the time, Robert Leband, it gives the local gossip as well as the price of corn and notes of local events.

Kate Greenaway, the author and illustrator of many children's books spent much of her childhood here and she has often referred to the time she spent in the village as a source of inspiration.

Averham
Map 4 ref D5

4 miles E of Southwell on the A617

Situated on the banks of the River Trent, this pleasant village, whose name is pronounced locally as Airam, is somewhat overshadowed by the nearby power station at Staythorpe. Though the village church, which dates from the 12th century is worth a visit, it is the vicars, and one in particular, which have put Averham on the map.

Joseph Walker was rector at Averham for 51 years before he was succeeded by his son Cyril in 1907. It was Cyril who built the **Robin Hood Theatre** in the grounds of the rectory. Starting life in 1913, as a private theatre for opera lovers, it has a fully equipped stage and orchestra pit, and boasted the rare advantage of being lit by electricity. In these hallowed walls, the late, great Sir Donald Wolfit, a local man born at nearby Balderton, gave his first performances.

Kelham
Map 4 ref D5

5 miles E of Southwell on the A617

Situated beside the River Trent the village grew up around the crossing which was probably upstream of the present bridge. An old farming community, it seems fitting that the estate village of Kelham should be used to develop the growing of sugar beet in this country when it was introduced during World War I. The experiment was successful and, in 1921, the Kelham sugar beet processing factory was opened. Now called the Newark factory, it is one of the largest and most up to date in Europe.

The present **Kelham Hall** is the third manor house to be built on the site and this monument to all that is best in Victorian architectural splendour was designed by architect, Sir George Gilbert Scott. Today, the hall is home to the Newark and Sherwood District Council but, in 1903, it was the home of the a group of monks led by Father Herbert Kelly. Becoming known as the Kelham Fathers, Kelly not only trained monks for missionary work but also was responsible for the planting of what has now become a fine collection of trees.

Upton
Map 4 ref D5

2 miles E of Southwell on the A612

Upton boasts a couple of very good pubs and its nine-pinnacled church is worthy of a visit too. As a point of interest, a famous son of the village was James Tenant, the man who cut the world renowned Koh-I-Noor diamond. But, perhaps, the most impressive building here is **Upton Hall**, a stylish Grecian villa with a central dome and elegant colonnade, built in the early 19th century. The hall is now the headquarters of the **British Horological Institute** and, inside, visitors can see the **National Exhibition of Time** - a fascinating display of clocks, watches, and other horological pieces.

When Francis West (who later became Bishop West) first came to Upton as its new vicar it was in the severe winter of 1947. With postwar fuel shortages, many people would retire to bed early and the new vicar was no exception, particularly as the vicarage was not only large but drafty. However, Francis West used the time to read through some 17th-century account books he had found in an ancient parish chest. Telling the story of everyday life in Upton around that time, the vicar later published *Rude Forefathers* which shed much light on just how the turbulent times of the Civil War affected the local community.

The French Horn

Lovers of fine food will be well advised, if they are in the area, to seek out **The French Horn**, a super inn and restaurant situated in Upton just off the main Newark to Mansfield road. Dating back to the 18th century, it was formerly a farmhouse then an alehouse and is now renowned throughout the area for its food. The restaurant seats up to 60 people and is found in the upper part of the building above the stables in what was the old hayloft. It really is a beautiful restaurant, the old wooden beams enhancing its character and cosy intimate atmosphere while the menu offers something to suit every palate. Open all day, for brunch mid-morning and light snacks in the afternoon in addition to the regular lunchtime and evening menu. It is best to book at peak times to avoid disappointment. The bar area with its log fire adds to the character of the place and its walls are adorned with the work of local artists Penny Veys and John Smith. *The French Horn, Upton, Nottinghamshire NG23 5ST Tel: 01636 812394*

Ollerton

The name of the village was originally Alreton or Allerton, meaning farm among the alders, and the trees still grow here along the banks of the River Maun. The village lies on the road from London to York (though now it is bypassed) and also on the roads from Newark to Worksop and Lincoln to Mansfield so, as a consequence, Ollerton developed as a meeting place for Sherwood Forest officials and the inns became staging posts during the coaching era.

Over the centuries the village was owned by several families including the Markham family. Staunch Catholics, the Markhams, along with their servants, were persecuted in the 16th century and their private hidden chapel can still be found in the roof of the present **Ollerton Hall**. The hall, which came into the hands of the Savile family in 1746, is now a Sue Ryder Home.

Ollerton Mill

Ollerton Mill is beautifully situated in a corner of rural England that has not changed for centuries. Standing on the same spot as an ancient mill, which was recorded in the Domesday Book, the building lies beside the River Maun on the edge of Sherwood Forest. The present owners, the Mettam family, came here in 1921 though they have been millers from many generations and their family history has been traced back to the 17th century when it was discovered that they had Kneesall Windmill.

The mill has recently been restored to working order and appears as it would have done some 300 years ago. Now a historic museum it is worth remembering that the mill is only open on Sundays but is well worth making a special visit. Through colourful displays the story of the mill's history, from Norman times to the present day, is told and an interesting video presentation shows the processes of grinding and milling that take place here.

The old millwright's workshop, which straddles the mill race, has been turned into a charming and delightful tea rooms. Open every day except Mondays, delicious freshly made scones, cakes, and light meals are always on the menu. *Ollerton Mill, Market Place, Ollerton, Newark, Nottinghamshire NG22 9AA Tel: 01623 822469/824094*

The **Ollerton House Hotel** was originally a private house but it became a pub around the 1950s. Since then the building has been extended to provide extra accommodation for the now separate restaurant and Ollerton House also retains its old off licence door at the front. Though Helen and Stephen Richardson have not been at the pub for very long (they came here in July 1997), they have quickly stamped their personality on the pub and it is fast becoming one of the most popular places in the district.

Ollerton House Hotel

The bar and lounge bar are both spacious and this is the place to come to to exchange gossip and enjoy a pint or two of the local beer. Lively and with a warm and friendly atmosphere, every Thursday evening is quiz night and there is always something going on each Saturday evening. The cosy restaurant, which is growing in popularity daily, offers a varied and extensive menu of freshly cooked dishes that change regularly. Those looking for overnight accommodation will be interested to learn that the Ollerton House Hotel also has six excellent rooms available on a bed and breakfast basis and children are welcome at all times. *Ollerton House Hotel, Wellow Road, Ollerton, Newark, Nottinghamshire NG22 9AP Tel: 01623 861017*

South of Ollerton

Rufford   *Map 1 ref C4*
1 miles S of Ollerton off the A614

Rufford Abbey was founded in 1146 by Gilbert de Gant as a daughter house to the Cistercian Rievaulx Abbey. However, during the Dissolution it suffered the fate of many religious houses and it came into the hands of the Earls of Shrewsbury and it was the husband

Rufford Abbey

of Bess of Hardwick, the 6th Earl, who, in the 16th century, turned the abbey into the country house seen today. The remaining ruins of the abbey are said to be haunted by the ghost of a giant monk with a skull-like face: there is written evidence in the parish register for Edwinstowe that a man died of fright after catching sight of this unholy visitor!

In 1626, the house was bought by the Savile family who lived here until the 1930s and it was they who carried out many of the improvements. Now in the hands of the County Council, the abbey's stable block houses an impressive craft centre while the restored 18th century orangery hosts modern sculpture exhibitions.

The grounds of the abbey, now the **Rufford Country Park**, are also well worth a visit and, as well as the nine formal gardens near the house, there also some hides where birdwatchers can overlook a portion of the lake which has been designated a bird sanctuary. In the grounds too lies an 18th-century corn mill, now home to a display of Nottinghamshire history, and two icehouses dating from the mid-19th century. As well as the majestic Lime Avenue, there is also the Broad Ride, at the southern end of which are several animal graves. Most were pets belonging to the family at the house but one grave is that of the racehorse Cremorne, the 1872 Derby winner.

Bilsthorpe   *Map 1 ref C5*
4 miles S of Ollerton off the A614
There was certainly a village here during the 9th century when the Danes were plundering the county though, now, there is little to see from those days. However, the hall, where Charles I is reputed to have hidden during the Civil War, still exists but it is now incorporated into a farm which stands opposite the village church.

Bilsthorpe remained a quiet farming community, as it had been for many centuries, right up until 1922 when a coal mine was sunk in the village by Stanton Ironworks. An explosion at the mine with a subsequent loss of life brought the vicar and the mine manager into a dispute over compensation. The manager, unwilling to pay out, built a wooden church away from the main part of the village and near to the temporary accommodation that was provided for the mine workers. Bilsthorpe continued to have two churches up until the nationalisation of the coal mines when the wooden church became the church hall.

Farnsfield   *Map 3 ref C5*
7 miles S of Ollerton off the A614
Traces of a Roman camp can be found in Farnsfield and there is also said to be the ghost of a Roman soldier who haunts one of village's pubs. More recently, the village was the birthplace of Augustus Charles Gregory. After emigrating to Australia, Gregory became

the first person to explore the country's interior and this earned him the name of Protector of the Aborigines.

Kirklington
Map 1 ref C5

6 miles S of Ollerton on the A617

Mentioned in the Domesday Book as Cherlington, this old village once kept many ancient customs. Centred around the village **Church of St Swithin**, the festivities were generally associated with the farming calendar. The church is partly Norman and any-one venturing inside will see that the pulpit has some small holes in its side that have been plugged with more recent wood. Their explanation is quiet extraordinary and dates from the early 19th century when a sporting rector would, during the week, have the pulpit removed from its base and transported to a nearby swamp. Here, he would lie in wait for wild duck which frequented the swamp and fire at the ducks through the holes in the pulpit's sides!

Archway House

Archway House, standing in 14 acres of grounds, dates back to 1917 but it is linked to the Arch and Toll House for the old Mansfield to Newark road which dates back to 1740 and can still be seen. The home of Erica and Colin McGarrigle, this is a wonderful bed and breakfast establishment which is certainly off the beaten track. The house is large by any standards and the three guest bedrooms are all on the first floor and offer glorious views over the well-tendered gardens and out over a golf course. The extensive grounds also contain a swimming pool and a lawn tennis court and, for the less energetic, there is also a croquet lawn.

Erica and Colin are charming people and offer all their guests superb hospitality, however long or short their stay. Breakfast is served in the outstanding dining room, complete with period furniture and delightful outlooks. Delicious evening meals can also be provided by prior arrangement and small meetings and conferences can be accommodated. *Archway House, Kirklington, Nottinghamshire NG22 8NX Tel: 01636 812070*

Caunton
Map 2 ref D5

7 miles SE of Ollerton off the A616

This ancient village was mentioned in the Domesday Book under the original spelling of the name, Calneton, which is sometimes still used locally today. The village Church of St Andrew was rebuilt by the Normans at the beginning of the 13th century but, by the 19th century, the building had fallen into such a state of disrepair that the altar, a wooden box, was only used as a resting place to the visiting curates hat and gloves.

A small and quiet farming community, the village was also the home of Samuel Reynolds Hole who became known as the Rose King - a title given to him by Tennyson. Before becoming Dean of Rochester, Hole lived at Caunton Manor as the squire and vicar and it was here that he began his extensive study of roses. By 1851, he recorded that he had over 1000 rose trees with over 400 varieties, a collection which was to make him the most famous amateur rose grower of all.

Cromwell
Map 2 ref E5

8 miles SE of Ollerton off the A1

The large, 17th-century rectory in the village is now home to the **Vina Cooke Museum of Dolls and Bygone Childhood**. Appealing to adults and children alike, there are all manner of children's toys on display but, perhaps the most fascinating are the handmade dolls which depict celebrities and famous historical characters.

Wellow
Map 2 ref C4

1 miles SE of Ollerton on the A616

This pretty conservation village is located on the site of an early settlement and it was once fortified by an earthwork and, on the western side, by Gorge Dyke. The remains of the earthwork can still be seen and villagers have retained the right to graze their cattle on enclosed land. The village green, once also used for cattle grazing, is now home to a permanent **Maypole** which is put to very good use during the annual May Day celebrations when the village also continues the tradition of crowning a May Queen.

Other notable features of this surprising village include a ducking-stool and stocks, and the 17th-century case clock in the 12th-century parish **Church of St Swithin**. The clock face was made locally to commemorate the coronation of Elizabeth II in 1953. Each year on the 19th September, the three church bells, which are between 300 and 400 years old, are rung in memory of Lady Walden.

Some 200 years ago she was paying a visit to Wellow and became lost in a local wood. Following the sound of the church bells, Lady Walden eventually found her way to the village and, such was her relief, that she left money for the bells to be rung forever on that day.

The Durham Ox is an attractive 17th-century former coaching inn which has been refurbished and extended over the years, yet still retains its individual character and charm. Since taking over in 1990, proprietors David and Julie Preston have created the friendliest of atmospheres. The interior is delightfully decorated, with smart comfortable seating, a stylish bar area, and walls adorned with traditional brasses. Customers are greeted with roaring log fires on cold wintry days and, in summer, great fun is had by all who attend the regular barbecue nights.

The Durham Ox

The Durham Ox has an excellent reputation for its food. David, a qualified chef who has been in catering since the age of 15, is now assisted by three further full-time chefs. The menu offers an extensive range of first class cuisine, as well as a variety of popular dishes in smaller portions for children. Children are most welcome at the Durham Ox, both in the new family room and in the well-equipped and safe-to-get-to garden area. David and Julie also provide free live entertainment every other Wednesday evening and on the last Sunday of every month. *The Durham Ox, Wellow, Nottinghamshire NG22 0EA Tel: 01623 86102666*

East of Ollerton

Laxton *Map 2 ref D4*

4 miles E of Ollerton off the A6075

This ancient village, mentioned in the Domesday Book, is unique as it is the only place in the country that has managed to retain its open field farming system. Devised in the Middle Ages, this system was generally abandoned in the 18th and 19th centuries when the enclosure of agricultural land took place and along with this many of the villagers' grazing rights.

The fields have been strip farmed here for about 1,200 years and the reasoning behind this was to ensure that farmers had an equal share of both good and poor land. With the dividing of the land, a farmer could have as many as 100 strips, which would have represented about 30 acres. By the 17th century, the strips were, on average, about half an acre in size but, with the advent of more efficient means of ploughing, this increased to three-quarters of an acre. The familiar three year crop rotation also ensured productive use of the land.

Laxton

Any stroll around this remarkable village is sure to take in some of the old farms and their outbuildings. The 18th century was a great time of rebuilding in Laxton and many of the houses display the patterned brickwork that was typical of the 1700s. The still visible stonework around the bottom of some buildings suggests that the foundations were of much older timber framed constructions.

Just north of the village, along a lane close to the church, is another fascinating aspect of Laxton's medieval history. This is the Norman motte or **Castle Mound** which lies almost hidden beneath the trees. At the beginning of the 12th century, the stewardship of Sherwood Forest moved to Laxton and the village became the administrative centre for the forest. As a consequence, the motte and bailey castle was one of the biggest in this part of the country and the village grew dramatically.

Over the years, however, the size and importance of Sherwood Forest dwindled and Laxton suffered a similar fate. Although no ruined keep or crumbling walls exist today, the castle earthworks are still the largest and best preserved in the county. All the information needed by the visitor on the history of this fascinating village can be found at the **Laxton Visitor Centre**.

Situated in this historic village is the magnificent **Dovecote Inn** owned by Her Majesty The Queen. The village is unique in its continued operation of a form of manorial government which has survived from medieval times and Laxton enjoys a legal status which permits an imposition on anyone abusing manorial law. Villagers meet at The Dovecote late in November or early December to appoint a jury which is then responsible for inspecting the fallow field in the next cycle. They tour the field left fallow for the past year then adjourn for lunch back at the Dovecote.

During the afternoon they then discuss the offences committed by farmers. A week later comes the Court meeting. An information centre is housed in the pub's old outbuildings which were converted and opened in 1986 and a video is also available. Laxton is the only open field village where 20th-century farming practices go hand-in-hand with medieval agricultural administration.

Formerly a farm, The Dovecote was turned into a pub in the mid-1800s. Today it provides food and drink seven days a week. As the inn is popular, booking is recommended for the 60 cover dining area on Friday and Saturday evenings and Sunday lunchtime. The menu is very comprehensive and offers home-cooked dishes to order, with the addition of numerous daily specials. There are also lots of exciting ales to choose from with five different bitters. To the rear of the pub is an excellent beer garden with an area catering for up to seven caravans or camping spaces complete with washing facilities and other amenities. *The Dovecote Inn, Laxton, Nottinghamshire NG22 0NU Tel: 01777 871586*

Lilac Farm lies on the outskirts of Laxton, just 10 minutes from the A1 and within easy reach of Newark, Lincoln, and Sherwood Forest. This charming farmhouse, last renovated in 1748 when the thatched roof was replaced by pantiles, is owned by Margaret and Reg Rose who offer excellent bed and breakfast accommodation with an English Tourist Board One Crown rating. This is a comfortable and homely house where all guests are welcomed as one of the fam-

Lilac Farm

ily. There are three cosy bedrooms, all with television, and children and small pets are also welcomed. A full and delicious farmhouse breakfast is served in the morning and an evening meal is available if booked in advance. Reg, an expert in local history, is a guide to Laxton Visitors Centre and is curator of the ***Laxton Heritage Museum***, housed in converted farm buildings at Lilac Farm. *Lilac Farm, Laxton, Nottinghamshire NG22 0NX Tel: 01777 870376*

North and South Collingham   *Map 2 ref E4*
11 miles E of Ollerton off the A1133
Originally a Saxon settlement which grew into the twin villages of North and South Collingham, they were, again, reunited in 1974. Lying close to the River Trent there has always been, until recently, the threat of flooding and, on the churchyard wall can be seen the water marks from long ago. The church building itself and the graveyard were built on a mound to save them from flood damage. Of most interest in the village is the Saxon cross which can be found at the northern end.

Girton
Map 2 ref E4

11 miles E of Ollerton off the A1133

The old part of this village lies along the banks of the River Trent and, until as recently as the 1970s, this area regularly suffered from flooding. So much so, in fact, that it was said that the people of Girton had webbed feet. Legend has it that one wet night the villagers were huddled together in the upper stories of their houses when, as the waters were rising, the church bell began to toll. The next day, after the flood had subsided, the villagers went to the church and found that cattle had congregated there, on the high ground, and that one cow had chewed through the bell rope!

Though the village **Church of St Celia** was rebuilt in 1876, it does contain the oldest ecclesiastical item in the diocese of Southwell: a late 8th century cross.

Sutton on Trent
Map 2 ref D4

9 miles E of Ollerton off the B1164

This village owes its existence to the River Trent, on whose banks it lies, and, at one time, Sutton on Trent was famous for basket-making and, in particular, for fishermen's baskets. In the late 19th century many people were employed in the industry and they came from far and wide to work here. One worker, it is recorded, came from Pittsburgh, USA!

The Leylands Guest House

The Leylands Guest House lies in the pleasant surroundings on the northerly outskirts of Sutton on Trent on the B1164 between the village and Weston. Though built only 5 years ago, the house was constructed from reclaimed materials and, along with the traditional design, this has given The Leylands a charming olde worlde feel with plenty of character. Owned and personally run by Val and Richard Walton, this is a warm and friendly guest house with the latest modern facilities. Accommodation is offered in three comfortable and cosy bedrooms, one of which has an en-suite bathroom. The full English breakfast is home-cooked and hearty as is the evening meal that is available by prior arrangement. With reductions for children, a guests' television lounge, and ample car parking this is a super place to stay. *The Leylands Guest House, Great North Road, Sutton-on-Trent, Nottinghamshire NG23 6QN Tel: 01636 821710*

Weston   *Map 2 ref D4*
7 miles E of Ollerton on the B1164

Situated along the old Great North Road, during the days of stage-coach travel, Weston was a busy place with several coaching inns. During this time, in the mid-18th century, a stagecoach footman, John Morris, upset at being in competition for his loved one, expressed his feelings by engraving a poem on the window of an inn. Engrossed in his work, Morris missed the coach on which he was supposed to be riding. As there was a heavy fine for missing a coach, the footman ran to catch up but try as he might he was no match for the team of horses and, so the legend goes, he ran himself to death.

South Clifton   *Map 2 ref E4*
11 miles E of Ollerton off the A1133

This pleasant village along the banks of the River Trent still has the remains of an old wharf where the coal from Derbyshire and Yorkshire was unloaded before being distributed throughout the surrounding area. The river here is still much used though the local fishermen now have to contend with water-skiers travelling up and down.

On the village green stands a young oak tree, planted in 1981, along with a plaque commemorating the achievements of a local farmer. Dusty Hare, who has lived in the parish all his life, has scored the highest number (7000) of points in Rugby Union Football and he was honoured with an MBE in 1989.

North Clifton   *Map 2 ref E3*
11 miles E of Ollerton off the A1133

The village, like its neighbour South Clifton, also lies on the east side of the Trent and is close to the border with Lincolnshire. The two villages are, however, quite separate, but they share the same church, dedicated to St George the Martyr, which lies between them.

The Pureland Meditation Centre and Japanese Garden offers a haven of peace for all ages who wish to come and experience the benefits of relaxation and meditation. Buddha Maitreya, a former Zen monk from Japan, has devoted the last 17 years to creating a Japanese garden and centre where all can come and seek refuge from the pressures of the 1990s.

The garden reflects the natural landscape of Japan with its large central pond, bridges, and a small pagoda where visitors can relax and meditate, among an abundance of flourishing plants and trees. Images are certainly conjured up of authentic Japanese gardens. The Buddha hopes that, after leaving, visitors will have a sense of inner peace and self-awareness and feel at one with nature. The garden is open Tuesday to Saturday from 13.00 to 17.30

sitting.....
beautiful peace
the world is pure consciousness
the Flow is Eternal Life
Divine Providence
crystallization is Ten Thousand Things

everything is sitting
tree is sitting
mountain is sitting
flower is sitting

Meditation is flower
is mountain
is tree

pure mind is all
land of bliss

Maitreya

The Pureland Meditation Centre and Japanese Garden

and Sunday and Bank Holidays 10.30 to 17.30 between April and October. The garden is closed on Mondays. Light refreshments are served. The centre is situated half way between Newark and Gainsborough, off the A1133. Buddha Maitreya teaches relaxation and meditation at the centre and is available for individual tuition and group relaxation and meditation. Group garden visits are welcome by appointment. *The Pureland Meditation Centre and Japanese Garden, North Clifton, near Newark, Nottinghamshire NG23 7AT Tel: 01777 228567*

Thorney
Map 2 ref E3
14 miles E of Ollerton off the A57
This small, quiet village was also the site of a gruesome murder which took place in 1805. A local labourer, Thomas Temporell, who was also known locally as Tom Otter, was forced to marry a local girl whom, it was claimed, he had made pregnant. Tom was so upset by the accusations and the enforced marriage that, in a frenzy, he murdered his bride on their wedding night. The story goes that he then took her body and left it on the steps of a public house in Saxilby, Lincolnshire. Caught and tried, Tom was sentenced to death with the extra penalty of gibbeting (the practice of hanging the offender's body in chains at the scene of their crime).

Darlton
Map 2 ref D3
8 miles NE of Ollerton on the A57
Within the village lies **Kingshaugh**, a name meaning king's enclosure, where King John is believed to have built a lodge and en-

Kingshaugh

closed some land for his own personal hunting in 1211. Abandoned as early as 1215, a 17th-century house now stands on the site. However, the history of the site goes back beyond the days of King John and excavations have revealed not only neolithic flints and Romano-British pottery but also extensive earthworks which go back to the Iron Age. Covering some 7 acres the banks and ditches were extended and used in Norman times when the site was first used as a hunting lodge. The house here today incorporates from medieval masonry within its walls.

Tuxford   *Map 2 ref D4*
6 miles NE of Ollerton on the A1

Very few buildings in the town are more than 300 years old because, in 1702, a great fire swept through Tuxford leaving few buildings standing in its wake. One survivor, however, was the 13th-century **Church of St Nicholas**, whose font is one of a few in the county which was installed within a couple of years of the Restoration in 1660.

To the south lies **Weston Mill**, a 19th-century windmill which is in a rather poor condition, whilst to the north lies the more impressive **Longbottoms Mill**. Also dating from the 19th century, Longbottoms Mill has retained most of its machinery in tact though it has not been a working mill for many years. Now restored and with a new cap and sails, the mill is occasionally open to the public.

The Newcastle Arms Hotel

The Newcastle Arms Hotel, found in the heart of the old market square, offers that traditional English hospitality typical of old coaching inns. Margaret Tudor, sister of Henry VIII, stayed here in 1503 on her journey north to marry King James IV of Scotland and to-day's visitors will receive no less a royal welcome! Traditional decor and antique furnishings, help create and elegant, yet informal and friendly atmosphere throughout the hotel. The comfortable bed-rooms are all en-suite and offer the full range of amenities. There is a fully licensed à la carte, French cuisine restaurant which has won the RAC award for outstanding food for three consecutive years. Excellent bar snacks and coffee are provided in the bar where both residents and nonresidents alike can relax. For those who are trav-elling for pleasure the Newcastle Arms provides an ideal base from which to discover the many leisure attractions if Nottinghamshire's Robin Hood Country. The businessman is also well catered for with a special lunch menu and full conference facilities. *The Newcastle Arms Hotel, Market Place, Tuxford, Nottinghamshire NG22 0LA Tel: 01777 870208*

Egmanton
5 miles E of Ollerton off the A1

Map 2 ref D4

The **Shrine of Our Lady of Egmanton** was a place of pilgrimage in the Middle Ages, then in 1896, the cult was revived by the 7th Duke of Newcastle. The exterior of the little medieval **Church of St Mary** is really quite modest but the interior, which the duke had refurbished, is a mass of colour, with the light from many tapers and candles giving it a mesmerising atmosphere.

The church is rich with other splendours too - an elaborately decorated and gilded organ, painted panels and pulpit, and many other religious objects. The shrine, which can be found on the north side of the chancel, houses the figure of the Virgin, surrounded by flowers and candles and protected by a canopy. In the Middle Ages, a local woman was said to have had a vision of the Virgin Mary, and this has consequently been a place of pilgrimage for centuries.

The person responsible for building Egmanton's motte and bai-ley **Castle** is not known but, as Roger de Busli held over 100 man-ors in Nottinghamshire, including the manor of Egmanton, it may well have been his doing. The motte, or mound, is exceptionally well-preserved and is some 20 feet high whilst, in places, the bank and ditch of the bailey can also still be seen.

Situated in Egmanton's main street is **The Old Plough Inn**, a traditional English free house of the highest calibre. It is well worth the detour to come and discover this wonderful hidden place, with its friendly atmosphere, warm, welcoming interior, and exposed oak beams. In addition to the fine selection of premium cask condition ales, the Old Plough Inn also boasts a restaurant where visitors can enjoy delicious dishes in a relaxed setting. The food is of the highest quality, only the freshest of ingredients are used, and everyone can be sure of getting good value for money and friendly, helpful service. In addition to the varied menu, a further selection of black-

The Old Plough Inn

board specials are available and are changed weekly. The restaurant is open from 19.00 until 21.30 Tuesday to Saturday, and from 12.00 until 14.00 from Wednesday to Sunday for lunch. *The Old Plough Inn, Main Street, Egmanton, Nottinghamshire NG22 0EZ Tel: 01777 872565*

CHAPTER SIX
North Nottinghamshire

North Leverton Windmill

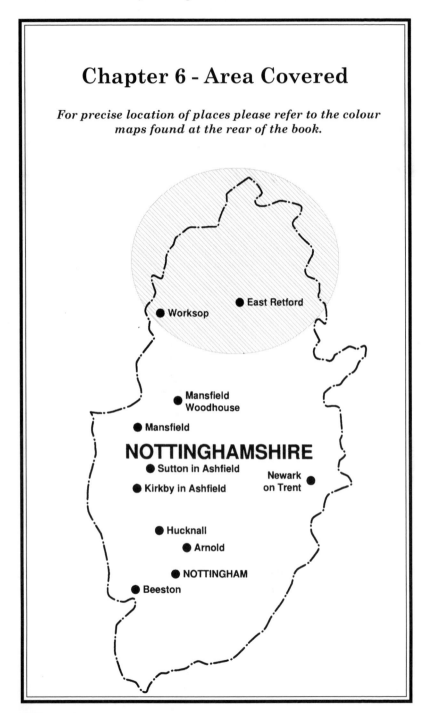

Chapter 6 - Area Covered

For precise location of places please refer to the colour maps found at the rear of the book.

● East Retford

● Worksop

● Mansfield Woodhouse

● Mansfield

NOTTINGHAMSHIRE

● Sutton in Ashfield

Newark on Trent ●

● Kirkby in Ashfield

● Hucknall

● Arnold

● NOTTINGHAM

● Beeston

6
North Nottinghamshire

Introduction

This northern area of the county is centred around the two old market towns of Worksop and Retford. The northern gateway to Sherwood Forest, Worksop, in the west of Nottinghamshire, is now very much an industrial town but, behind the 19th- and 20th-century buildings there is much of the old town to be seen. Retford, to the east, is much less industrialised and it has served the surrounding rural villages for over 500 years.

From this quiet and, basically, rural area the origins of the United States of America can be traced. During the late 16th century, in the villages of north Nottinghamshire, those opposed to Elizabeth I's policy of Church government began to form themselves into the Pilgrim movement, held together in their firm belief in the freedom from State control of religious matters. The members of the Separatists group increased and they held their meetings in secret to escape persecution.

By 1608, their persecution by James I became so great that the Pilgrim Fathers, as they were later to be called, fled to Holland. Some years later, in 1620, they sailed from Plymouth to America on board the *Mayflower*, landing at Cape Cod. From there they sent out an expedition to find a suitable settlement and, at a place now known as Forefathers Rock, in Plymouth, the New World was established.

Retford

The town has grown in importance over the centuries, from the granting of its market charter by Henry III in 1246, to the prosperity bought to it by the railway and canal links. The town is made up of *East Retford* and *West Retford*, each lying on opposite banks of the River Idle. Of the two, West Retford is the older and it is presumably this parish which received a mention in the Domesday Book as Redforde. East Retford was established in 1105 on the other side of the river as a place where tolls could be collected from people make the river crossing. An attempt was made, in the 18th century, to make the river navigable from Retford to Bawtry but this was unsuccessful though the diversion of the Great North Road through the town, in 1766, did bring more prosperity to Retford.

The *Market Square* was laid out in the late 18th century after the rerouting of the Great North Road through the town. Still at the heart of the life of Retford today, with a bustling market every Thursday and Saturday, the square is surrounded by many of the town's most noteworthy buildings, including some fine Georgian houses. The grand and rather chateau-like *Town Hall* was built in 1868 to replace the Georgian hall which stood on the northeast side of square.

Outside the Town Hall can be found the *Broad Stone*, which is probably the base of an old parish boundary cross. Tradition has it that during the times of the plague in Retford, in the mid-16th and mid-17th centuries, coins were placed in a pool of vinegar in the hollow in the top of the stone so prevent the disease from spreading whilst trading was taking place at the market.

In the northwestern corner of the square is an archway which leads down to the River Idle. Bearing the inscription "JP Esquire 1841" the archway once led to the gardens of John Parker who lived in a nearby house which is now a business premises. A close inspection of the garden wall will reveal that it has a hollow curve. This was caused by heat passing along the wall to warm the fruit trees which were grown in its shelter.

Cannon Square now occupies the site of East Retford's ancient market place and it is also home to one of Retford's more unusual attractions: a Russian cannon. Dating from 1855 and weighing over 2 tons, the cannon was captured by British soldiers at Sebastopol and was brought to Retford at the end of the Crimean War. The townsfolk paid for its transportation and, in 1859, after arguments raged about its siting, it was placed in the square and named the Earl of Aberdeen after the incumbent Prime Minister. During World War II the cannon was threatened with being melted down to help the war effort and it was only saved after a Retford gentleman bought it and hid it until the war was over.

Not far from Cannon Square is, reputedly, the oldest chemist's shop in the country still on its original site. Opened in 1779, **Norths Chemists** first belonged to a local vet, Francis Clater, whose books on animal medicine and treatment were bestsellers for over 100 years.

One of the town's most infamous visitors was the highwayman Dick Turpin and several historic inns still stand as a reminder to the great days of the stage coach. Another man who stood and delivered here, though in a more respectable fashion, was John Wesley, who conducted many of his open air meetings in East Retford.

When in Retford, it is well worth visiting the **Bassetlaw Museum** in Amcott House, Grove Street. This imposing late 18th-century town house was once the home of the Whartons, the woollen drapers; Sir Wharton Amcotts, MP for the Borough of East Retford; and the Peglers, the local industrialists. It was extensively restored and opened as a museum for the District of Bassetlaw in 1986. The

Bassetlaw Museum

house is noted for its finely executed internal plasterwork and elegant wrought iron staircase, which the restoration has returned to their full Georgian splendour. The museum has a distinct local emphasis, with displays of local archaeology, civic, social and industrial history, and fine and applied art. There is also a continuous programme of short term exhibitions which are of interest to visitors and residents alike. Bassetlaw Museum is open Mondays to Saturdays from 10.00 to 17.00; admission free. *Bassetlaw Museum, Amcott House, Grove Street, Retford, Nottinghamshire DN22 6JU Tel: 01777 706741*

After many years as a collector of colour box miniatures and teddy bears, Louisa opened *Courtyard Collectables* just off Retford's main street. What was once a hobby has been turned into a thriving business that has gone from strength to strength since she opened at the beginning of 1997.

Courtyard Collectables

The shop has two large display windows that are dressed with a selection of the wide variety of stuffed bears and animals, ornaments, statuettes, and other objects d'art which can be found within. Pride of place inside Courtyard Collectables is given to the Teddy bears. They come in all shapes and sizes and, as well as stocking well-known makes such as Steiff, Merrythought, and Deans, there are numerous traditional and more modern bears from which to choose. Well laid out and with plenty of room to admire the colourful displays, customers will also find Enchantica Dragons, Piggin' Pigs and much more. This is the ideal place in which to find the perfect present for young and old and is certainly an interesting shop not to be missed. *Courtyard Collectables, 3 Glasby Square, New Street, Retford, Nottinghamshire DN22 6EP Tel & Fax: 01777 705779*

The Market Hotel, formerly known as the Cattle Market Hotel, stands on the historic site of the old cattle market with the now disused Harwich to Liverpool Railway running alongside it, in the Ordsall district of Retford. To one side of the hotel where there were once piggeries and a tack salesroom, there is now a magnificent function room, ideal for wedding receptions and private parties.

The Market Hotel

This delightful hotel has been in the Brunt family for over 20 years and is now run by Ray and his son, Graham. Ray prides himself on the wide range of real ales he stocks in the cosy bar, having no less than 14 different varieties at any one time. He is also justifiably proud of the superb and extensive menu which includes a wide range of mouthwatering fish dishes - watch out for the size of the Scarboro' haddock! *The Market Hotel, West Carr Road, Retford, Nottinghamshire DN22 7SN Tel: 01777 703278*

South and East of Retford

Eaton   *Map 2 ref D3*
2 miles S of Retford on the A638
This small hamlet was once part of the estate of the Dukes of Newcastle which incorporated several other nearby villages. The land known as **Eaton Wood**, now managed by the Nottinghamshire Wildlife Trust, was mentioned in the Domesday Book as an area of pasture woodland and some of the ancient ridges and furrows can still be seen. A wood of mainly ash, elm, and hazel with some oak, Eaton Wood is more important for the plant life it sustains such as moschatel, yellow archangel, and several orchids.

Gamston
Map 2 ref D3

3 miles S of Retford on the A638

In the time of the Normans it was recorded that there were three mills and two manors in this small village but since then it has been part of the estate the Dukes of Newcastle. In 1782, when the candlewick factory opened in the village it was the first of its kind in the world and local men and women were employed round the clock. This venture however closed in the mid-19th century and the ground breaking factory buildings were demolished in 1854.

East Drayton
Map 2 ref D3

6 miles SE of Retford off the A57

A rural village, overlooking the River Trent, East Drayton is fortunate in being designated a conservation area and several of the older buildings in the village centre have undergone restoration work to bring them back to their former glory. A quiet and peaceful village, it was the birthplace of the 17th-century architect Nicholas Hawksmoor. He left the village at the age of 18 to begin his career and during his life he worked with both Christopher Wren and Vanbrugh on many projects including the Royal Naval College at Greenwich.

Grove
Map 2 ref D3

2 miles SE of Retford off the A638

From Grove Hall there is a secluded, paved path, called the Private Walk, which leads up to nearby **Castle Hill Woods**. It was built for a lady of the hall so that she could walk to the woods in privacy whilst she was pregnant. The woods which once covered a much larger area contain, in a moat field, the site of a Roman camp.

North Leverton
Map 2 ref D2

5 miles E of Retford off the A620

The correct name for this village is North Leverton with Habblesthorpe which has been described in editions of the Guinness Book of Records as the longest multiple place name in England. The two villages were united in 1884.

The 12th-century village Church of St Martin is reached via a bridge over a stream whilst the Wesleyan Sunday school, near the crossroads, was built in 1838. However, by far the most outstanding feature in the village is the **Windmill**, built in 1813 when it was known as the Subscription Mill. Despite rebuilding work over the years, it remains an attractive sight and it is also the only working windmill in the county. The windmill is open to visitors most days except Tuesdays and freshly ground floor can also be bought from the mill.

Sturton-le-Steeple *Map 2 ref D2*
5 miles E of Retford off the A620

Sturton is a corruption of the word Stretton, which means the town on the street, and the village lies on the Roman road known as Till Bridge Lane which ran from Lincoln to Doncaster. The origin of the second part of the name is immediately obvious as the village is approached. The splendid tower, with its 12 impressive pinnacles, rises above the houses and is quite the highest point for miles around in this flat landscape. It was formerly part of the church, which was destroyed by fire in 1901.

North of Retford

Clarborough *Map 2 ref D2*
2 miles NE of Retford on the A620

Many footpaths cross **Clarborough Hill** and, from the top, there are splendid views over Lincolnshire, Derbyshire, and south Yorkshire. The Chesterfield Canal, which runs close by the village not only provides more interesting walking along the towpath but also there is good angling.

The Retford to Gainsborough railway line runs through the village and there is a very attractive nature reserve, **Clarborough Tunnel**, along the railway cutting and above the tunnel here. A mix of dense woodland, scrub, and grassland, little has been disturbed here since the railway was built in 1849 and the reserve is well known for the various species of orchid found growing on the limey soil.

Clayworth *Map 2 ref D2*
4 miles N of Retford on the B1403

The **Chesterfield Canal**, which lies close to the village, is Nottinghamshire oldest canal. Completed in 1777 and running through the north of the county, it was once a busy waterway carrying all manner of goods between Derbyshire and the River Trent at West Stockwith. Today, it is the sole preserve of pleasure craft and, particularly in the summer, is once again well used.

In this tiny hamlet is a rare gem to discover in **The Blacksmiths Arms and Wiseton Restaurant**. Dating back to the 17th century, it was formerly a smithy and a license was granted in the early 19th century. Visitors will find a very warm welcome at the Blacksmiths which has been refurbished to the highest standards. This is very much a restaurant first and an inn second. Original beams and timber work is now enhanced by designer furniture and fabrics. The superb Wiseton Restaurant offers excellent à la carte and

The Blacksmiths Arms and Wiseton Restaurant

table d'hôte menus providing a varied choice of the finest cuisine, accompanied by an excellent wine list. The tables are beautifully laid out with the finest crystal and crockery, enhancing still further the dining experience. This is certainly one place people are sure to return to time and again. *The Blacksmiths Arms and Wiseton Restaurant, Clayworth, near Retford, Nottinghamshire DN22 9AD Tel: 01777 818171*

Grange Farm stands in 38 acres of scenic countryside close to the Yorkshire and Lincolnshire borders. This charming Queen Anne farmhouse dates back to 1700 and is, today, the home of Julia and David Wagstaff-Myers, who offer bed and breakfast accommodation in a choice of two comfortable rooms. The couple breed horses and, in the fields around the house, there are often foals to be seen. There is also ample stabling at the farm as well as a menage and field with jumps so that visitors staying here can also bring their horse. The ideal holiday base for horse riders, not only is there some excellent hacking country on the doorstep but Julia and David also offer tuition.

Guests who are not inclined to ride will also be able to enjoy the countryside in the company of horses as David is happy to take visitors on a carriage ride in a Victorian Landau which he also uses for weddings and other special occasions. The premises are surrounded by the Chesterfield Canal were fishing is available though guests will need a rod licence and walks along the banks of the canal link with the Trent Valley Way. After a day out in the open Grange Farm is a lovely place to come home to with open fires and

Grange Farm

beautifully period furnished rooms. The large garden is also open to guests and the secluded patio the perfect place to sit on a summer's evening. Grange Farm, however, is not terribly suitable for younger children. *Grange Farm, Town Street, Clayworth, near Retford, Nottinghamshire DN22 9AD Tel: 01777 816367*

Mattersey
Map 2 ref C2

5 miles N of Retford off the B6045

At the end of the village a rough lane leads down to the ruined **Mattersey Priory**, which was founded in 1185 for the Gilbertine Order; the only monastic order to be founded solely by the English. Never a wealthy establishment, when the house was founded there were only six canons; though the numbers fluctuated over the years, by the time of the Dissolution there were only five living here. The original priory buildings were destroyed by fire in 1279 and the remains seen today are of the dormitory, the refectory, and the walls of the Chapel of St Helen. The site is rarely visited by tourists and, with the River Idle nearby, it is a quiet, picturesque, hidden spot that is well worth finding.

Everton   *Map 2 ref C1*
5 miles N of Retford off the B6045

Lying in a wide horseshoe created by the meandering River Idle and with the Chesterfield Canal across the open end, Everton is almost an island. In the centre of the old village there is a row of terraced houses which are said to be haunted by the ghost of a dog. Thought to have lived here in the early part of the 20th century, the dog's ghost scrabbles at doors and runs across the hallway of his master's house.

Gringley on the Hill   *Map 2 ref D1*
6 miles NE of Retford on the A631

Standing on a ridge, but still only 82 feet above sea level, this village has commanding views over Yorkshire, Lincolnshire, and Nottinghamshire. The best vantage point is **Beacon Hill**, on the east side of the village, which, of course, was used for beacon fires and, though it is likely that this was once the site of a prehistoric settlement, excavations have revealed no evidence for this claim.

The village **Church of St Peter and St Paul** dates from the 12th century and one of the church bells is, rather oddly, dated to the time of the Commonwealth. During this period bells and other decorative items were considered frivolous and were generally dispensed with but, as the parish records show, the people of Gringley did not adhere to such ideas and they also celebrated Christmas which was then illegal!

Gringley Hall

Gringley Hall, the home of Ian and Dulce Threlfall for the last 18 years, is a lovely, large country house surrounded by two acres of beautiful gardens. In 1914, the Hall became an isolation hospital for children with TB. In the grounds the old school room, where the children with this crippling disease were taught, can still be seen. The hall did not revert back to a private house until 1957. There is also a tennis court and croquet lawn for those who enjoy this entertaining and sometimes cruel game.

From this wonderful house, Ian and Dulce offer luxury bed and breakfast accommodation in three comfortable bedrooms, each with private facilities. Spacious and well decorated and furnished the rooms have large beds and one even has a dressing room, a reminder of more genteel days. Children are always welcome and there is a kennel available for dogs. *Gringley Hall, Gringley on the Hill, Nottinghamshire DN10 4QT Tel: 01777 817262 Fax: 01777 816824*

Misterton   Map 2 ref D1
9 miles NE of Retford on the A161

This village owes much of its early prosperity to Charles I when, in the 17th century, he appointed the Dutch engineer, Sir Cornelius Vermuyden, to drain the marshes in the area. Famous for the work he did in building the complex drainage system in East Anglia, Vermuyden and his Dutch workforce again worked to provide excellent arable fields on the reclaimed land which became known as the Isle of Axholme. As a consequence of this work, many of the farms date from this time.

Another great addition to life in Misterton came in 1777 with the opening of the Chesterfield Canal. Linking the village with other market towns, it was also found that the clay cut to build the waterway was ideal for brick making and so a brickworks were opened along the banks of the canal.

Surrounded by old cottages and farm buildings, the village church has a rather stumpy spire, which rises from its tower without a parapet, that is known as a broach spire. One notable feature inside the church can be found in the Lady Chapel. This is the stained glass window designed by John Piper, which depicts the Crucifixion using the symbols of hands and feet and the Sacred Heart.

North Wheatley   Map 2 ref D2
4 miles NE of Retford off the A620

This village, surrounded by farmland, is famous for its strawberries which are sought after for their delicious taste and excellent quality. North Wheatley is also home to a peculiar brick house, dated 1673, and with the Cartwright arms above its brick porch. Known as the **Old Hall**, all the external features, including the vase-like decorations, have been made from bricks and it is a much loved subject by local artists.

Rose Cottage, the home of Gwen and Michael Bennett-Curtis, is tucked away in the quiet hamlet of **Bole** (just to the northeast of North Wheatley) and it is surrounded by an acre of fruit, vegetable and flower gardens. Of the couple, Gwen is the gardener and in the 17 years that they have been at the cottage, she has established a wonderful garden which yields all manner of fruit and vegetables. Not satisfied to leave her labours there, Gwen then heads for the kitchen to preserve the fruits and make home-made wine.

Rose Cottage

Those lucky enough to stay in this charming bed and breakfast establishment can take advantage of Gwen's excellent home grown fare at dinner, as well as some of her wonderful jam at breakfast. The accommodation too is of a high standard, with three en-suite bedrooms available. For that special occasion Gwen and Michael will arrange a Murder Mystery weekend for up to eight friends. Nearby Nottingham is famous for its Goose Fair and Gwen and Michael have the old parchment deeds dating from 1650 that state that the cottage was, at one time, purchased for one shilling. Those were the days! *Rose Cottage, South Street, Bole, near Retford, Nottinghamshire DN22 9EJ Tel: 01427 848572*

Worksop

Despite the unattractive modern houses that lead into the town, there are some fine Georgian buildings to be found in Bridge Street. One of the real attractions of Worksop is the **Priory Gatehouse** which is best approached from Potter Street, where the full glory of the 14th-century building can be seen. Its great niches house large and beautifully carved statues and the immense entrance is rather reminiscent of a cave opening. Originally the portal to a large Augustinian monastery, the gatehouse together with the Church of St Mary and St Cuthbert is all that remains. There is also a wayside shrine, which makes it a unique ecclesiastical attraction. Today, the upper floor of the gatehouse houses an art gallery and exhibitions are put on here regularly.

The first canal to be built in Nottinghamshire was the ***Chesterfield Canal*** which runs from Chesterfield in Derbyshire to the River Trent. Some 46 miles long, work on the canal was begun in 1771 and it took 6 years to complete under the supervision of John Varley, the deputy of the great canal engineer, James Brindley. In the mid-19th century the canal was taken over by the Sheffield and Lincoln Junction Railway, who, in 1863, decided to cease maintaining the waterway and allow it to run down. The collapse of one of the canal's two tunnels, at Norwood in 1908, hastened its decline by effectively cutting off Chesterfield from the rest of the waterway.

During the canal's heyday, in the early 19th century, it was indeed a busy waterway and many buildings lined its route, particularly through Worksop. ***Pickford's Depository***, spanning the canal in the centre of the town, was typical of this time. The trap doors in the stone archway over the canal were used for the loading and unloading of the cuckoos, as the narrowboats on the Chesterfield Canal were called.

A recent acquisition by the National Trust, ***7 Blyth Grove***, is unusual, quite unique and also well worth a visit. The familiar looking house and a million pounds was left to the Trust by William Straw in his will and the Trust was surprised to find upon inspection of the Edwardian semidetached house that they were actually stepping back in time. Inside, everything had been preserved from 1932 when William Straw senior, a grocer and seed merchant in Worksop died. Seven years later his wife died and the two sons, William and Walter, lived a bachelor existence at the house. Walter, who took on the family business, died in 1976 and his brother, William who,after first teaching at the City of London College, eventually returned to look after the house and died in 1990.

In all those years, little had changed: their parents' bedroom was closed up and everything left as it was; a 1932 calendar still hung on the wall; their father's hats were still perched in the hall; and his pipes and tobacco pouch were ready by the fireside. Now the Trust have a unique record of social history of those times with a display of items that reflects life as it was in the 1930s and the earlier decades of this century.

One remnant of the northern part of Sherwood Forest lies near the town. **Hannah Park Wood**, which covers some 14 acres, is mainly made up of oak and beech but there is also a small section of yew trees.

Worksop Museum, found in Memorial Avenue, is housed in a large purpose-built gallery within the library and museum provided by the Carnegie United Kingdom Trust which was opened in 1938. Within the museum are small exhibitions relating to the history of Worksop and the neighbouring area of landed estates known as the Dukeries, together with a larger display on the Pilgrim Fathers

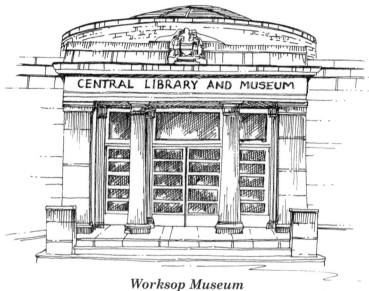

Worksop Museum

whose roots lay in north Nottinghamshire. Presiding over the Pilgrim Fathers Exhibition is a life-size model of Pilgrim Elder, William Brewster, one of the leaders of the movement. Worksop Museum and Gallery is open Mondays to Saturdays from 09.30 to 18.00 (13.00 on Thursdays and Saturdays). *Worksop Museum, Public Library, Memorial Avenue, Worksop, Nottinghamshire S80 2BP Tel: 01909 501148*

Miss Poppy's Coffee Shop can be found in the centre of the town on the first floor above Eyre's furniture shop and overlooking the market. A definite cut above the average coffee shop, Miss Poppy's, which is owned and personally run by Shiela and Bob, is more like a small restaurant. Since coming here three and a half years ago, Shiela and Bob have completely refurbished the premises and, not surprisingly, there is a poppy theme running through the coffee

Miss Poppy's Coffee Shop

shop that is subtle rather than over powering.

Everything served here is freshly made on the premises by Bob, whose culinary skills are in no doubt: there are home-made scones, cakes, and pies that really make the mouth water. As well as the usual coffee shop fare, Miss Poppy's also has an extensive menu of hot and cold light lunches and snacks that are ideal at any time of day. Shoppers and visitors to Worksop will welcome the friendly and peaceful atmosphere of this establishment and, as well as taking the opportunity to rest here a while, there are also magazines and papers for customers to read. Children are not forgotten and there is a corner set aside for them with plenty of toys to keep them amused. *Miss Poppy's Coffee Shop, Eyres of Worksop, Market Place, Worksop, Nottinghamshire S80 1HD Tel: 01909 488958*

In the heart of Worksop, across from the market, **The Lion Hotel** has been looking after the needs of weary travellers for over 400 years. Although completely modernised, it still oozes with charm and character from years gone by. Luxuriously furnished and decorated throughout, there is an excellent lounge bar, an elegant restaurant, a function room, and 32 wonderful bedrooms, all en-suite and equipped for maximum comfort.

The Lion Hotel

This is definitely a place fit for a king but frequented by all walks of life, with welcoming and friendly staff soon putting guests at their ease and ensuring their stay is pleasurable and relaxing. *The Lion Hotel, 112 Bridge Street, Worksop, Nottinghamshire S80 1HT Tel: 01909 477925 Fax: 01909 479038*

North of Worksop

Carlton-in-Lindrick   *Map 1 ref C2*
2 miles N of Worksop on the A60
This village's name has a delightful meaning - the freedmen's enclosure in the limewood. It does, however, consist of two villages, North Carlton and South Carlton, and it is the latter which is the elder. Believed to have been a Saxon settlement, South Carlton, or Carlton Barron as it was also called, is home to the village church. With its massive Saxon tower, the church is quite awe inspiring as it soars above the village and, in Church Lane, is the ***Old Mill Museum***, housed in a converted 18th-century water mill. On display are some unusual linen pictures, which were used by the Victorians as educational material, as well as farming implements and mill machinery.

Oldcotes

Map 1 ref C2

5 miles N of Worksop on the A634

A pretty brook runs through the village and there is also an unusually styled farmhouse with Gothic windows. The Roman Catholic **Church of St Helen**, with its lovely interior, was built in 1869 by the owner of nearby Hermeston Hall. Whilst the excavations for the church's foundations were being made, the remains of a Roman villa were unearthed complete with a mosaic floor which is thought to have been laid at around the same time as Hadrian's Wall was being built.

Situated in the village, very near to Nottinghamshire's border with Yorkshire and a few minutes drive from the A1, is the outstanding **King William IV**. Owned by Whitbread Sherwood Inns, it is one of their Brewers Fayre range and has been managed for the past 18 months by Paul and Barbara Ayres. Formerly an old coaching inn, it was refurbished completely and became a Brewers Fayre in 1990. The decorations and furnishings are really excellent combining the best of the old and lots of memorabilia with modern facilities in a very pleasing atmosphere.

King William IV

The King William is open seven days a week and the restaurant areas can seat 180, so there is no need to book here. In addition to the standard Brewers Fayre menu there are at least six delicious daily specials offered which usually includes vegetarian dishes. All ales are kept in top condition and Boddingtons, Trophy, and Manchester Gold are always available. Indoor and outdoor children's play areas are excellent as is the access and assistance for the disabled. *King William IV, Blyth Road, Oldcotes, Worksop, Nottinghamshire S81 8HU Tel: 01909 730225*

Harworth
Map 1 ref C1

7 miles N of Worksop on the B6463

Dating back to the era of the Saxons, Harworth is unique amongst Nottinghamshire mining villages in that it has wide curved streets and crescents rather than the usual rows of terrace houses. The explanation for this enlightened design probably comes from the fact that coal was not discovered here until after World War I.

Bircotes
Map 1 ref C1

8 miles N of Worksop off the B6463

The twin village of Harworth, it was here that local estate house, Serlby Hall, home of the Galway family, stood. As well as opening a hospital in Harworth during World War I, the family also endowed another house on their estate as a school for the children of both villages. Today, the school, Brailsford House, has been converted into a residential home.

Scrooby
Map 1 ref C1

8 miles NE of Worksop on the A638

Scroppenthor existed here before 958, the year that King Edgar granted the land rights to Oscytel, the Archbishop of York. But Scrooby's greatest claim to fame is through William Brewster, who was a founder member of the Pilgrim Fathers.

It was at Cambridge that Brewster's radical ideas on religion were formed and his spell in the Netherlands, with its toleration of religious views, gave him a new perspective. He returned to England, settling in Scrooby, and, in 1598, he was summoned before the ecclesiastical court for poor church attendance, which was to lead him on the path to Separatism and the freedom of religion from control by the State. His outspoken views, for the time, eventually forced him to resign his post and he became outlawed for his ideas. Imprisoned for a short time in Boston, Lincolnshire, Brewster made his way back to Amsterdam. After some years he returned, again, to England and, in 1620, he left again on board the *Mayflower* with a group of like-minded people. He was by now an elder of the Separatist Church and the group later became known as the Pilgrim Fathers. Brewster and his colleagues founded a colony in Plymouth, New England and he died in America, in 1644, at about the age of 77.

Though Brewster is by far the most famous of the Pilgrim Fathers there are two other interesting gentlemen who played an equally important role. One of the youngest members of the movement, William Bradford, who was born into a prominent Yorkshire family in 1589, had to withstand his families opposition to his beliefs. To escape their disapproval and the penalties for not attending his local church, Bradford joined the group at Scrooby. It was another gentleman, Richard Clyfton, who persuaded Bradford to travel to America on board the *Mayflower* and it is through his writings that the early days of the work of the Fathers is known. Clyfton was, himself, the rector of **Babworth Church** (a few miles south of Scrooby) and it was his inspirational addresses which laid the foundations of the movement. He was forced out of his post and became their pastor. The 15th-century church was used by the Pilgrim Fathers as their place of worship and it is justly proud of its historic connections.

Babworth Church

For such a small village, Scrooby has a wealth of other interesting features. There is a stone walled pinfold near the churchyard where straying cattle or sheep were rounded up and released on payment of a fine. The Pilgrim Fathers Inn dates back to 1771, although it was originally called The Saracen's Head. The Monks Mill, which stands on the old course of the River Ryton, is now a private dwelling and despite the name it has never had any close associations with a monastery.

Scrooby was also the scene of a particularly grisly murder. In 1779, a shepherd from North Leverton called John Spencer murdered the local tollbar keeper, William Yealdon, and his mother Mary. Caught in the act of trying to dispose of the bodies in the river nearby, Spencer was later executed at Nottingham Assizes. His body was then taken back to Scrooby to hang in chains from a gibbet that had been specially erected near the scene of the crime.

Blyth   *Map 1 ref C2*
5 miles NE of Worksop on the A634

The approach to the village is dominated by the great tower of the **Church of St Mary and St Martin** which looms above Blyth and is one of the most important Norman buildings in the country. The eight tall pinnacles are linked by a delicate tracery of stone that gives a surprising grace to the 900 year old tower. Although the first impression is of a Gothic structure, the Norman windows give its origins away and the church epitomises the French love of dignity and simplicity with its rather solemn air.

There are many other buildings of distinction in the village, including a handsome stable block and the former rectory which is surmounted by a cupola. Among the redbrick Georgian houses there are also a number of coaching inns which act as a reminder that Blyth was once an important staging post on the Great North Road.

At the far end of the village is **St John's Hospital**, which was originally founded as a leper hospital in the 12th century and later converted into a school. The former schoolhouse stands on a diamond shaped island of grass, obviously dating back to a time when these poor unfortunates (the lepers not the pupils!) would have been kept isolated from the villagers.

Just to the southwest of the village lies **Hodsock Priory** and its beautiful **Gardens** which stands within its own parkland and meadows. Although this would seem to be the perfect setting for a medieval monastery, no priory ever stood here. The present house was built in 1829 in the Tudor style to complement the marvellous 16th-century gatehouse. The gatehouse is approached across an ancient rectangular moat and, within this area, the gardens have been laid. The southern arm of the moat was made into a small lake around 1880. The gardens are well known for their shrub roses and the owners, Sir Andrew and Lady Buchanan, are more than happy to welcome the public into their lovely grounds.

Between Blyth and the nearby village of Styrrup, to the north, lies the **Tournament Field**. Dating back to the Middle Ages, the field was one of only five in the country to be granted a royal licence.

Barnby Moor

Map 1 ref C2

6 miles NE of Worksop on the A634

One of Nottinghamshire's smallest villages, at one time Barnby Moor lay on the Great North Road and it had several fine coaching inns. One of the village inns, the Blue Bell, became so busy with stage coaches passing through in the early 18th century that one traveller remarked that it was so busy that he could not find any room in the inn at all. Now called the Olde Bell Hotel, the local hunt meets here every Boxing Day. As the village was also isolated, it attracted many highwaymen who could plunder the coaches then make an easy get away.

Tourist Information Centres

Centres in **bold** are open all the year around.

Newark

The Gilstrap Centre, Castlegate, Newark, Nottinghamshire
NG24 1BG Tel: 01636 678962 Fax: 01636 612274

Nottingham

1-4 Smithy Row, Nottingham NG1 2BY Tel: 0115 977 3558
Fax: 0115 9772421

Ollerton

Sherwood Heath, Ollerton Roundabout, Ollerton
Nottinghamshire NG22 9DR Tel: 01623 824545

Retford

Amcott House, 40 Grove Street, Retford, Nottinghamshire
DN22 6LD Tel: 01777 860780

West Bridgford

County Hall, Loughborough Road, West Bridgford
Nottinghamshire NG2 7QP Tel: 0115 977 3558 Fax: 977 2421

Worksop

Worksop Library, Memorial Avenue, Worksop, Nottinghamshire
S80 2BP Tel: 01909 501148 Fax: 01909 236277

Index

V

W

The Hidden Places Series

ORDER FORM

To order more copies of this title or any of the others in this series
please complete the order form below and send to:

Travel Publishing Ltd,7a Apollo House, Calleva Park
Aldermaston, Berks, RG7 8TN

	Price	Quantity	Value
Regional Titles			
Channel Islands	£6.99	....	....
Devon & Cornwall	£4.95	....	....
Dorset, Hants & Isle of Wight	£4.95	....	....
East Anglia	£4.95	....	....
Gloucestershire	£6.99	....	....
Heart of England	£4.95	....	....
Lancashire & Cheshire	£4.95	....	....
Lake District & Cumbria	£4.95	....	....
Northeast Yorkshire	£6.99	....	....
Northumberland & Durham	£6.99	....	....
Nottinghamshire	£6.99	....	....
Peak District	£6.99	....	....
Potteries	£6.99	....	....
Somerset	£6.99	....	....
South East	£4.95	....	....
South Wales	£4.95	....	....
Surrey	£6.99	....	....
Sussex	£6.99	....	....
Thames & Chilterns	£5.99	....	....
Welsh Borders	£5.99	....	....
Wiltshire	£6.99	....	....
Yorkshire Dales	£6.99	....	....
Set of any 5 Regional titles	**£25.00**	....	....
National Titles			
England	£9.99	....	....
Ireland	£8.99	....	....
Scotland	£8.99	....	....
Wales	£8.99	....	....
Set of all 4 National titles	**£28.00**	....	....
	TOTAL	_____	_____

**For orders of less than 4 copies please add £1 per book for
postage & packing. Orders over 4 copies P & P free.**

PLEASE TURN OVER TO COMPLETE PAYMENT DETAILS

The Hidden Places Series
ORDER FORM

Please complete following details:

I wish to pay for this order by:

Cheque:	☐	Switch:	☐
Access:	☐	Visa:	☐

Either:

Card No: ☐☐☐☐ ☐☐☐☐ ☐☐☐☐ ☐☐☐☐

Expiry Date: ☐☐ ☐☐

Signature: ....

Or:

I enclose a cheque for £ .... made payable to Travel Publishing Ltd

NAME: ....

ADDRESS: ....

....

....

....

POSTCODE: ....

TEL NO: ....

Please send to: Travel Publishing Ltd
7a Apollo House
Calleva Park
Aldermaston
Berks, RG7 8TN

The Hidden Places Series
READER REACTION FORM

The Hidden Places research team would like to receive reader's comments on any visitor attractions or places reviewed in the book and also recommendations for suitable entries to be included in the next edition. This will help ensure that the *Hidden Places* series continues to provide its readers with useful information on the more interesting, unusual or unique features of each attraction or place ensuring that their stay in the local area is an enjoyable and stimulating experience.

To provide your comments or recommendations would you please complete the forms below as indicated and send to: **The Research Department, Travel Publishing Ltd., 7a Apollo House, Calleva Park, Aldermaston, Reading, RG7 8TN.**

Please tick as appropriate: Comments ☐   Recommendation ☐

Name of *"Hidden Place"*:

Address:

Telephone Number:

Name of Contact:

Comments/Reason for recommendation:

Name of Reader:

Address:

Telephone Number:

The Hidden Places Series
READER REACTION FORM

The Hidden Places research team would like to receive reader's comments on any visitor attractions or places reviewed in the book and also recommendations for suitable entries to be included in the next edition. This will help ensure that the *Hidden Places* series continues to provide its readers with useful information on the more interesting, unusual or unique features of each attraction or place ensuring that their stay in the local area is an enjoyable and stimulating experience.

To provide your comments or recommendations would you please complete the forms below as indicated and send to: **The Research Department, Travel Publishing Ltd., 7a Apollo House, Calleva Park, Aldermaston, Reading, RG7 8TN.**

Please tick as appropriate: Comments ☐   Recommendation ☐

Name of *"Hidden Place"*:

Address:

Telephone Number:

Name of Contact:

Comments/Reason for recommendation:

Name of Reader:

Address:

Telephone Number:

The Hidden Places Series
READER REACTION FORM

The Hidden Places research team would like to receive reader's comments on any visitor attractions or places reviewed in the book and also recommendations for suitable entries to be included in the next edition. This will help ensure that the *Hidden Places* series continues to provide its readers with useful information on the more interesting, unusual or unique features of each attraction or place ensuring that their stay in the local area is an enjoyable and stimulating experience.

To provide your comments or recommendations would you please complete the forms below as indicated and send to: **The Research Department, Travel Publishing Ltd., 7a Apollo House, Calleva Park, Aldermaston, Reading, RG7 8TN.**

Please tick as appropriate: Comments ☐   Recommendation ☐

Name of *"Hidden Place"*:

Address:

Telephone Number:

Name of Contact:

Comments/Reason for recommendation:

Name of Reader:

Address:

Telephone Number:

Map Section

The following pages of maps encompass the main cities, towns and geographical features of Nottinghamshire, as well as all the many interesting places featured in the guide. Distances are indicated by the use of scale bars located below each of the maps

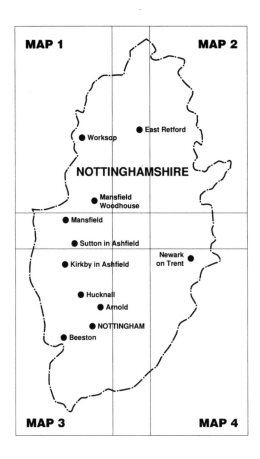

These maps are small scale extracts from the *Shires of Middle England Official Tourist Map,* reproduced with kind permission of *Estates Publications.*

Notes

Notes

Notes

Notes

Notes

Notes

Notes

Notes

MAP 1

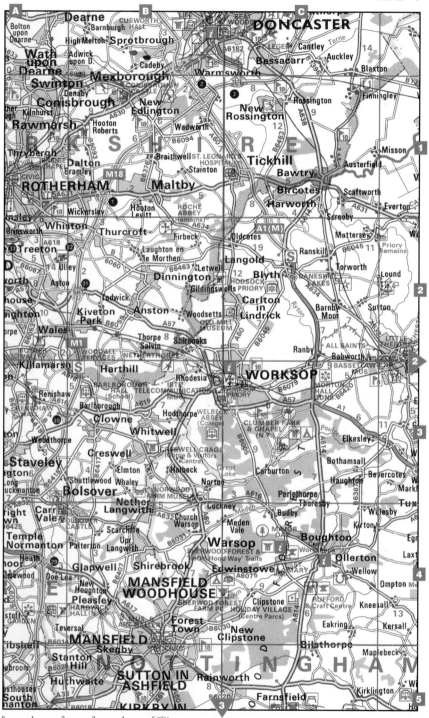

MAP 2

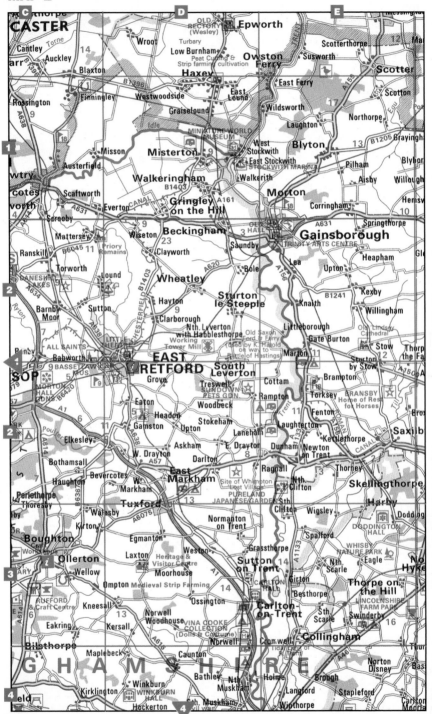

MAP 3

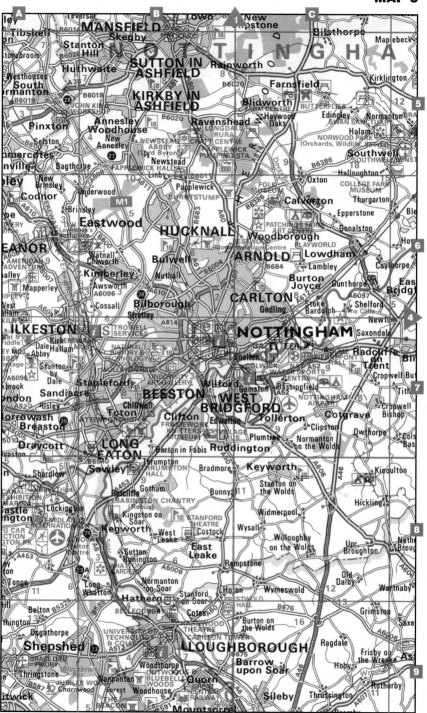

MAP 4

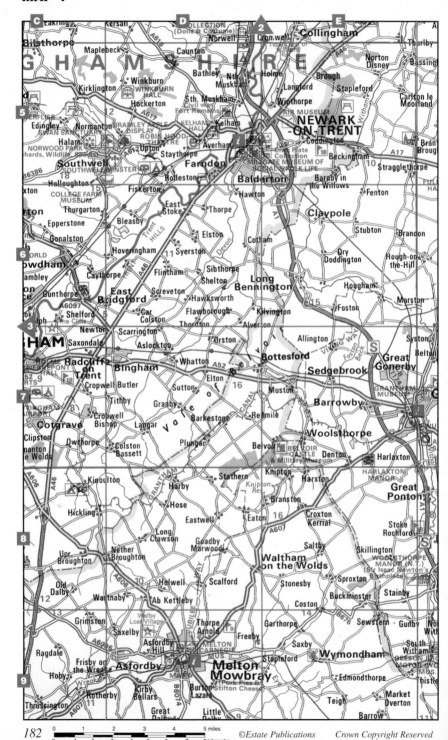

0   1   2   3   4   5 miles
0   1   2   3   4   5   6   7   8 kilometre

©Estate Publications   Crown Copyright Reserved